LOOK BEFORE YOU LEAN:

HOW A LEAN TRANSFORMATION GOES BAD—

A CAUTIONARY TALE

By

EMPLOYEE X

Cover art design by Zoko

ACKNOWLEDGEMENTS

This book could not have been written without the help of...nay, *would not* have been written without the help of my wife, Mrs. X, who kept telling me to go into work when I didn't want to because there was a story to be told unfolding there. Also, I'm indebted to my friend and lean guru Michael Ballé, who's not all together happy with everything I've written here, but who was nonetheless open minded and open hearted in counseling me through a lean journey unlike the ones he imagines for his clients. Also, to my co-workers--the veterans of course--the open floor plan they designed for us turned into a foxhole, and in the best tradition of foxholes forged us into a band of brothers...and sisters. Finally, to Scott Adams--I discovered *Dilbert* while the story I chronicle here was developing. I know he's been around forever, but perhaps you have to find unhappiness in your job before you find Dilbert. In any case, I subscribed to the strip and began every day with a much needed laugh and state of amazement at how this guy who probably hasn't had to work in an office for about 30 years still manages to "get" what goes on there. At the end of this book I offer some free advice to all those trying to get the modern workplace right. But here's a free tip for anybody who runs a company—prominently post the daily Dilbert strip right up there with your notices about worker safety, whistleblower protection, and harassment. Nothing I can think of will keep you and your employees saner than a little Dilbert in the morning.

DEDICATION

To *Angela*, the muse in spite of herself

VOICE FROM THE FACTORY FLOOR

Living is easy with eyes closed
Misunderstanding all you see
It's getting hard to be someone but it all works out
It doesn't matter much to me
Let me take you down,
'Cause I'm going to Strawberry Fields

If your local high school had a dropout rate of over 90%, it would be a national scandal. If Harvard Business School had a dropout rate of over 90%, it would cease to exist. So how, one wonders, does Lean,[i] the hot business methodology of the past two decades, continue to thrive when companies that sign up for it have been dropping out at a rate of more than 90%? [ii] There are people, even among Lean's most ardent advocates, who have conscientiously tried to deal with this daunting statistic. In this book I will try to help them and those tantalized by the allure of Lean by detailing as much as possible the Lean implementation I witnessed roll out at the company where I was employed for nearly 15 years. Although my company is only at the end of the second year of a consultant-driven, five-year Lean transformation, I'd say that chances are better than even that it will ultimately join the swelling ranks of companies that started and then quit Lean.

For readers unfamiliar with Lean, let me quote from the consultancy group that brought Lean to my company: "Put simply, lean achieves continuous improvement through people. It enables a process or business to realize its true performance potential through the fundamental use and application of various tools to see waste and eliminate waste."

That brings to mind one of my favorite passages from Walter Isaacson's biography of Steve Jobs. Isaacson reports that Jobs had a bootleg of the Beatles multiple recording sessions for "Strawberry Fields Forever" as the great musical group of our time struggled to get it to their liking. Jobs would play the tape for his managers to help create the company culture he wanted to foster at Apple. Quoting Jobs, Isaacson writes:

> "'It's a complex song, and it's fascinating to watch the creative process as they went back and forth and finally created it over a few months,' said Jobs. 'They

kept sending it back to make it closer to perfect. The way we build stuff at Apple is often this way. Even the numbers of models we'd make of a new notebook or iPod. We would start off with a version and then begin refining, doing detailed models of the design, or the buttons, or how a function operates. It's a lot of work, but in the end it just gets better, and soon it's like, Wow, how did they do that?!? Where are the screws?'" iii

I love the irony that a song with the theme "Nothing is real and nothing to get hung about" would help pave the way for the second richest company in the world. However, and more to the subject of this book, Jobs in effect took "the waste" from the Beatles—their outtakes—and used it to model his company culture. (Lean advocates will point to Jobs's statement that he kept sending back work until it was made perfect as an example of how he embraced the Lean principle of "continuous improvement," but the truth is that Steve Jobs was lean in body only.) I don't think I'm taking Lean too literally here as to what it regards as waste. I don't wish to get too far ahead of my narrative, but successful enterprises abound that were built on "waste" (welcome to the sausage factory, folks). And surely Jobs's invitation to his top people to sit around listening to discarded music tracks would strike some as "waste," though it all led to considerably more than waste. So there seems to be a foundational weakness in Lean's obsession with realizing business potential by eliminating waste.

Yet, Lean has proven irresistible to many companies. It has become for American business leaders what the Cabbage Patch Kid once was for children—they all want it and will pay any price to get it. Serious students of Lean have plumbed more sophisticated reasons for the failure of so many Lean implementations, but I would submit just for starters here that one of the simplest explanations is that, like the Cabbage Patch Kid, the novelty soon wears off and the company, like the child, is no longer amused.

Lean or otherwise, American captains of industry have always had a weakness for the shiny new things consultants dangle in front of them. The often hard, hostile landscape of American capitalism has been remarkably hospitable to a long cavalcade of traveling medicine shows driven by management consultants purveying nostrums disguised as pet theories and systems.

Lean, the nostrum *du jour*, has attempted to transform itself from its early incarnation as lean manufacturing, with firm roots in the Toyota factory environment, to an all-embracing, one-stop solution for all your business management needs. Before examining how that has led to an enormous and risky overreach—at least in terms of the company I worked for—a little historical perspective is in order.

Charles Bedaux, the godfather of American management consultants, started out in life, coincidently enough, working for a pimp on the streets of Paris around 1906. The pimp was teaching Bedaux everything he knew when he was murdered, forcing Bedaux to take his raw skills to the US where he soon became the major salesman for the pioneering scientific management studies in time and motion of Frederick Winslow Taylor and Frank and Lillian Gilbreath, respectively. As a self-styled efficiency expert, Bedaux began spreading the notion to industry that humans could be effectively turned into cogs in the manufacturing machinery by carefully calibrating their various motions to a stopwatch.

Bedaux's success, in the face of fierce labor union opposition, spawned a national boom in the business of advising other businesses how to conduct their business. It ushered in the great consultancy convergence, which gathered force throughout the 20th century and roared into the 21st. It's currently a 4-bilion dollar industry and growing, with more than 700,000 management consultants in the US at last count.

Bedaux's reputation for promoting industrial efficiency came to the attention of The Third Reich, which asked him to oversee the liquidation of Jewish businesses in Nazi-occupied France. (The Nazis, of course, knew a thing or two about efficiency, and their demise suggests that efficiency at times might be an overrated virtue.) The time and motion gospel that Bedaux preached has provided the foundation for generations of management consultants ever since.

The roll call of hot, new scientific management theories is a fascinating study in ephemera, demonstrating that hardheaded business people are as prone to fad and fashion as your typical teenager. Geoffrey James, of CBS *Moneywatch*, summed up some of the more notable of these fads with an irreverent set of thumbnails. Here are a few excerpts:

Six Sigma

"The theory: The idea is to improve the quality of your processes by identifying and removing the causes of defects. You assign various people different colored 'belts' (like a karate class) based upon their expertise in the Six Sigma methodology. You also get a series of defined steps and quantifiable financial targets.

"The reality: It creates a hierarchy of 'belted' experts who run around the company pretending that they know how to do other people's work better than the people who do the work. Endless meetings ensue, with little or no effect. The consulting firm who's implementing the Six Sigma walks away with a fat paycheck.

"The result: Wasted time and wasted effort. According to one quality control expert quoted in Fortune magazine, 'of

58 large companies that have announced Six Sigma programs, 91 percent have trailed the S&P 500 since.' On the other hand, it's spawned an entire industry of 'consultants' who make a living sucking productivity out of your firm.

"*Core Competency*

"The theory: Focus on the one thing that your firm does better than anyone else. That will make your strategy difficult for competitors to imitate and keep your organization from wasting time doing things that they're not very good at.

"The reality: Most organizations, like the managers that run them, are about as self aware as a turnip. As a result, they seldom know what they're really good at. In many cases, organizations think they're good at something but are actually successful for some completely different reason.

"The result: Core competence generally ends up as a kind of myth that keeps a company locked into doing what it was successful at doing in the past. As a result, companies that focus on their core competence soon find that they have competitors running rings around them.

"*Management by Objectives*

"The theory: Define objectives within an organization so that management and employees agree to the objectives and understand what they are in the organization. Then compare the employee's actual performance with the standards set and agreed upon.

"The reality: Everyone spends hours making plans for the future. When the future actually happens, it ends up looking nothing like it was originally expected. As a result, everyone ends up either doing something that might have worked a year ago or doing something that wasn't in the original plan and then spends extra effort making it look as if they were performing to the plan.

"The result: Lots and lots of out-of-date planning documents and precious little to show for it. Success rate in the typical company is supposedly around 6% percent." [iv]

There have been numerous such management fads, and each one raises the same inescapable question: if any of them were as good as advertised, why the need for the next new thing? This is no idle question. It is in fact the most anti-capitalist question you can ask—even more anti-capitalist than why the hell shouldn't all the workers of the world unite. That's because even the workers of the world get the logic behind reinventing the wheel and rebranding it as a circle, a hoop, or an annulus. It's called job creation.

And the first object of management consultants is job creation—their jobs. Now there's nothing wrong with this. It's as human and necessary as eating. We all need to put food on the table. That's what the people who hire management consultants do, too, though they spend so much time consuming their own marketing materials that they lose sight of this truth and come to believe they really are selling nutrition or romance or safety or peace of mind or whatever ideal their advertising people have attached to their product or service. (In the outrageous documentary, *The Queen of Versailles*, Richard Siegel tries to inspire his sales staff by telling them they're not just selling timeshares, but saving lives—like doctors, firemen, and policemen do—because stress is a killer and vacations relieve stress.) Somehow, otherwise smart folks—entrepreneurs themselves—overlook the salient fact that outside consultants are entrepreneurs too, and you are their market base. Their business is to make money off your business. And if they help you do better business in the process...well, hey, that's icing on their cake.

This is why consultants like to sell you on the idea that they're your partners (and let's have a moment of silence for the death of that once noble word). The astute business exec knows very well what the word partner means and knows that a central element of it is shared risk. There is no shared risk in consulting. Unlike a pizzeria or express mail service, you pay the consultant regardless of what they deliver. And if what the consultants promised never materializes in terms of actual results—not process, but results—the only risk the consultants face is that they won't get a second chance to take your money.

As it happens, I've been married for more than four decades to a woman who's had a 30-year career as an outside consultant. She's spoiled me...and not just with her cooking and housekeeping but with the way she conducts her business. Whenever she's hired by a company to come in as an outside consultant, the first thing she does is ask for a list of employees who will be affected by her training so she can talk to at least some of them and find out what their needs are. She also puts a very high value on repeat business, so it's never hit and run with her. Yes, she, too, is in it for the money, but she's made a point of making sure her clients get their money's worth.

If your consultant is as intent on customer satisfaction as my wife is, you can tell right off because the consultant is treating you as its customer and not trying to bullshit you about being your partner. There is no sleight-of-hand to make you believe that *your* customers are their customers. Again, outside consultants are not invested in your customer's satisfaction no matter what they tell you. You are the only one in this so-called partnership who's ever at risk of losing your customers. And you should make sure that the consultant bears a similar risk in losing you as a customer by insisting that your relationship is as customer to vendor, and not a partnership.

If the consultants come in to your sausage-making plant and sell you on the idea of running your conveyor belt left to right instead of right to left and filling the skins from the back rather than the front and calling the whole new process The Total BS Management System, then that's what you bought. Unless you're a very shrewd negotiator, you probably didn't get the consultants to guarantee that your sausages will at least taste and sell better when they're done.

There does appear to be a glimmering of such shrewdness given recent reports of companies actually writing guarantees into their contracts with consultants...much as they might with the contractor who replaces the roof on the company headquarters. If the new roof springs a new leak...they fix that too or you get your money back. Why does this common sense principle not apply to consultants? It could be that it's often difficult for a company shopping for a consultant to step back and see itself as a buyer of product, rather than as a seller of one. But the company that fails to do that when shopping for a neatly packaged new company culture puts itself at great risk of losing not just time and money, but the company's way as well.

Following this long, baffling corporate tradition of forking over hundreds of thousands of dollars for advice from outsiders who'd never spent a day working in our industry, my company took such a risk. Unfortunately, before buying into Lean, my company, like others so smitten by its surface attractions, wasn't as keen as it should've been in following the oldest rule in the business of buying and selling: *caveat emptor*—buyer beware. It's not that our company leaders blindly made an expensive, long-term commitment to the consultants who would bring a major Lean presence through our doors. The company sent a 25-member delegation to tour a site where our prospective consultancy firm chose to highlight one of its successes. The delegation came back with glowing reports. But within the first year of our Lean transformation, it became clear through much of the company that no one had fully grasped all that we had bargained for.

This book is a chronicle of that year—and as much beyond as my continued employment there would allow. It does not aim to be an exposé of Lean. There is no smoking gun here that will bring a sudden halt to the mad rush of American business to embrace the Lean principles. In Lean parlance, I'm simply trying to "stop the line" of that mad rush by reporting what I observed from the "factory floor" while working for a company that had built a sterling global reputation for nearly a century.

Why our leadership chose to make the wholesale commitment to Lean that it did is open to conjecture. Although I was by no means privy to the inside data or meetings that led to it, my personal conjecture does not include greed, venality, or ignorance. But there is a fourth motivator of bad business decisions that may very well have been the key factor: fear.

There had been speculation about gathering global forces that posed an imminent threat to the company's standing. Given that the company's standing has been at the top of its industry, that's made the bet our leaders made on Lean very high risk. Without benefit of a parallel universe, no one will ever be able to tell if going Lean—and all the money and effort that entailed—helped us maintain our #1 standing. However, if the company eventually falls from #1, it will be evident globally that betting on Lean had been a losing proposition.

In his essential book *Thinking, Fast and Slow* (which will be mined throughout this book for antidotes to some of the nostrums dispensed by the Lean practitioners at our company), Nobel Prize winner Daniel Kahneman warns that CEOs of relatively sound companies do themselves no favors by panicking in the face of uncertainty. According to Kahneman, a company with its fundamentals in order—and ours was surely that—can and should allow time and luck, more reliable aids than any faddish business methodology, to see it through tough times.

Paul Levy, former CEO of Beth Israel Deconess Medical Center in Boston who saw Lean principles literally save his hospital, remains a passionate advocate for Lean at his perceptive and mercifully objective blog, "Not Running a Hospital." I don't know if the consulting firm he refers to in the following passage is the same one that set up shop at my company, but the similarities are as intriguing as the results of their handiwork are infuriating. Levy writes:

> "If there were a form of medical malpractice lawsuit that I would like to encourage, it would be against those consulting firms that promise hospitals that they will teach them how to 'do Lean.' I recently encountered a hospital in which a well known international consulting firm did it this way: Assemble 25 top level managers for a week-long off-site seminar, teaching them all the Lean terminology and getting them ready to do Lean projects. Then keep one or two of your consultants in residence for a few months to provide aid and comfort to the managers as they attempt to run rapid improvement events in areas of the hospital chosen by somebody as 'high priority' areas needing cost savings. Then leave behind your 'trained' cadre of managers to carry on— which they cannot or will not do. Charge

the hospital several hundred thousand dollars for this 'service.' But not before you have given Lean a bad name and, worse, have caused it to be associated with layoffs...

"...Lean... is a long-term philosophy of corporate leadership and organization that is based, above all, on respect shown to front-line staff. There are two essential aspects, training front-line workers to be empowered and encouraged to call out problems on the 'factory floor,' and training managers to understand that their job is to serve those front-line workers by knowing what is going on the front lines and responding in real time (when problems are fresh) to the callouts." [vi]

I've never worked on an actual factory floor in my life, but I feel free to claim the factory floor as the metaphor for the point of view of this book since my place in our company hierarchy is about at the factory floor level. My qualifications otherwise are limited to a few items on my résumé--I've spent more than 30 years doing all manner of corporate editorial for companies ranging in size from sole proprietorship to Fortune 500, and I've had some experience as an outside consultant myself in delivering writing seminars internationally for my wife's company. So, though I do not come to the writing of this book with an MBA or executive experience, I also don't have an ideological agenda, a pet theory, or a gimmick to sell. Nor do I have an axe to grind. It is common to smear writers of such books as this one as disgruntled employees. It's a typical and transparent tactic for marginalizing critical voices. Of course, happy employees don't write books like this. But then again happy spouses don't file for divorce and happy soldiers don't march to war. So being disgruntled is not exactly a disqualification for bringing a critical perspective to most any subject; often disgruntlement helps motivate and sharpen it.

This book is primarily, in the aggregate, a cautionary tale for those contemplating Lean for their businesses or those who work for a company that is trying to make a Lean transformation. This cautionary tale, however, is missing the scary event that such tales depend upon for full dramatic impact. There is no point at which the big, bad wolf huffs, puffs and blows the house down. My company does not go bankrupt, its stock does not plunge, workers do not resign *en masse* (though there are significant and troubling resignations). These typical headline-grabbing developments do not dominate this tale. Nonetheless, if wasting company time, money, and morale count for anything, this tale should provide the reader with chills aplenty.

Before I get to my warnings about others, however, I want to offer a warning about me because I really do trust in transparency. Writing about a study in which participants were exposed to various pieces of information in a legal dispute, Daniel Kahneman writes:

> "...Participants who saw one-sided evidence were more confident of their judgments than those who saw both sides. This is just what you would expect if the confidence that people experience is determined by the coherence of the story they manage to construct from available information. It is the consistency of the information that

matters for a good story, not its completeness. Indeed, you will often find that knowing little makes it easier to fit everything you know into a coherent pattern." vii

That's me—I do not know the whole story of my company's Lean adventure. I did not have full access to all the relevant material or meetings, nor am I an investigative reporter. But what I do know I've done my best to fashion into as coherent a narrative as possible with as consistent and honest a handling of the facts as I saw them. And that right there is far fuller disclosure about my limits than our Lean consultants ever offered my company about theirs.

I've framed the chapters ahead in terms of classic fairy tales. Fairy tales I should note were originally created to impart valuable lessons, rather than put children to sleep. I believe that imparting these lessons is a service not just for those companies contemplating Lean and their employees who will have to be the subjects of a Lean transformation, but for the legitimate Lean community, which out of pragmatism, politics, or professional courtesy is allowing their brand to be tainted by the spread of what one legit Lean advocate terms "lame Lean."

Contrary to conventional wisdom in the business world, the decision to go Lean is by no means a no-brainer and shouldn't be treated that way. In the words again of Paul Levy, "Lean is not for everybody." Allow me to add this to that: Bad Lean is not for anybody.

HANSEL & GRETEL

When four weeks had gone by, and Hansel still continued thin, she was seized with impatience and would not wait any longer. "Hola, Gretel," she cried to the girl, "be active, and bring some water. Let Hansel be fat or lean, tomorrow I will kill him, and cook him."

If you can recall the story of Hansel and Gretel before Hollywood turned it into a big budget shoot 'em up filled with monsters and gore, you know that it's the tale of a simple woodcutter who allows his second wife to make the biggest decision of his life about the two children he had with his dearly departed first wife. The woodcutter is a lot like a company CEO facing typical business problems of low cash flow and high overhead. Only in the woodcutter's case the low cash flow is affecting how much food he can put on the table, and overhead manifests itself as his two loving children—Hansel and Gretel. And the stepmother is much like the outside business consultant who comes in and tells the woodcutter that the only way to survive is to go lean—cut waste by taking those two unproductive little mouths out into the woods and leaving them there.

Let's stretch the analogy just a bit by calling the candy-covered cottage Hansel and Gretel come upon in the deep dark woods Toyota Corporation. Lean manufacturing is inextricably linked to Toyota. And for many companies wandering lost in the wilderness of the modern global economy, Toyota is very much a seductive candy-covered cottage. The Toyota brand has long been associated with so many qualities that consumers desire—reliability, value, economy, style. (For the record, our family owns two Toyota products, so I'm not immune to the lure of the brand.) What company seeing Toyota's success wouldn't say, "I want what they're having." And thus it is that many consultants who peddle Lean trade heavily on the Toyota connection. They repeat the name Toyota like a mantra, so prospects for Lean intervention can easily come to believe that they're buying Toyota's success rather than a methodology that may or may not be right for their particular business.

It is the stuff of entrepreneurial legend that Toyota, a giant of the automotive world, grew out of the humble loom business. Through the first half of the 20th century this fascinating metamorphosis could be called history's most dramatic period of *continuous improvement* if that core Lean concept had predated it. But the changes came first, forced on Toyota by events outside its inner sanctum and control—mainly a global economic crisis and a world war. Following the war, Toyota tried to meet the demands of producing a cheap car for an island nation devastated by war. But many of its efforts produced crippling labor strikes leading to the resignation of company president Kiichiro Toyoda in 1950. Lean zealots tend to put Bondo over this stretch of Toyota history. They would like you to believe that the path of Toyota's continuous improvement was unbroken from the time the legendary Taiichi Ohno was made machine shop manager in 1947 and instituted the changes that would become the foundation of the Toyota Production System (TPS) and ultimately Lean, which included:

- Rearrangement of machines from process flow to product flow

- End of one man one machine and start of multi-process handling
- Detail study of individual process and cycle times
- Time study and motion analysis
- Elimination of "waste" concept
- Reduction in work in process inventory
- In-process inspection by workers
- Line stop authority to workers

But the strikes and the resignation *followed* those innovations, and the critical next step in Toyota's evolution didn't happen until the company settled its dispute with its workers by virtually promising them lifetime jobs in exchange for going along with the program that would become the foundation of Lean. For all the benefits of Lean manufacturing (which are real) and all the success of Toyota that is due to Lean (also real), the favorable terms for the workers of the strike settlement was a major factor in allowing Toyota's fortunes to soar over the next half century.

In a comprehensive history of relations between workers and management in the worldwide auto industry, Beverly Silver of Johns Hopkins

University provides an assessment of Toyota's success that is free of Lean bias. She writes:

> "...When output began to expand in the 1950s, the assemblers avoided hiring new permanent workers, and instead adopted a policy of shifting work out to suppliers. 'The primary reason for [this shift to] subcontracting,' according to Smitka (1991:7), was 'to avoid renewed conflict with militant labor unions . . .' By following a strategy of expanding output, not through vertical integration, but through a widening reliance on subcontracting, Toyota increased output fivefold during 1952-57 while its workforce rose only 15%. (Smitka 1991: 2). This reliance on outside suppliers allowed the automobile assemblers to guarantee permanent employment to their own workers.
>
> "At first, the workers (and profits) at subcontracting firms provided the buffer that protected workers (and profits) at the main assembly firms. However, by

the 1960s, the contracting system had grown into a multilayered pyramid in which the primary subcontractors (those who sold directly to the assemblers) resembled the assemblers themselves, in terms of the use of advanced technology and the wage levels and employment security offered to their workers. The role of 'buffer' in recession fell to a larger group of secondary suppliers (who sold to the primary suppliers) and tertiary suppliers (who sold to the secondary suppliers) (Smitka 1991).

"This multilayered subcontracting system has allowed the Japanese automobile assemblers and their primary suppliers to develop relatively cooperative relationships with their employees, based on a commitment to lifetime employment and rising wages with age and tenure. They have therefore been able to minimize the costs associated with labor unrest since the upheavals of the early 1950s. This, in turn, has been a central component explaining the competitive success of the Japanese automobile industry on a world-scale since the late- 1960s." [viii]

As Lean is not responsible for all of Toyota's success, neither is all of Toyota's sterling reputation simply due to good practices and products. Like many successful companies, Toyota heavily relies on effective public relations—both of the direct and indirect kind. Thus, the Prius buys the company a lot of goodwill among America's progressive, environmentally conscious consumers. Its strategic dispersal of factories throughout the American South buys it a lot of goodwill in places where labor unions are not popular. And its heavy lobbying expenditures buy the company a lot of influence among the nation's politicians. Out of self-regard, Prius owners ignore Toyota's gas-guzzling Tundra and the still considerable carbon footprint of their precious hybrids. Out of self-interest, Southerners ignore the fact that they get paid 6% less yearly than their northern counterparts and thus drain jobs from the North. And Toyota's efforts to prevent Congress from passing legislation to mandate better gas mileage for all cars passes under the public's radar as American car manufacturers get cast as the villains in keeping the country dependent on foreign oil.

At this point, the attentive reader will cry out, "So wait a minute. How then can you suggest that Toyota is this big, mouthwatering house in the middle of the wicked scary woods?" Well, we must remember from the Hansel and Gretel tale that the confectionary cottage in the woods wasn't all that it was cracked up to be. Likewise, Toyota is not all that it is cracked up to be. As I write this, the company has just been hit with a record fine, as reported on CNN.com:

> "Toyota Motors has agreed to pay a record $17.4 million to the National Highway Traffic Safety Administration for problems that led to a 2012 recall in one of its Lexus models.
>
> "That's the largest fine allowed by law for a single investigation. Toyota once had among the best reputation for vehicle quality and safety but it has been dogged by significant recall problems over the last three years. It has already announced the recalls of more than 10

million vehicles worldwide for various problems so far this year.

"In 2010, Toyota paid a total of $48.8 million as a result of three separate investigations into pedals being caught in floor mats, sticky pedals and steering relay rod problems. Those recalls caused Toyota to briefly stop selling many models as it addressed problems, and its sales plunged in the wake of the negative publicity about the safety issues." [ix]

In his official statement on the first wave of recalls to hit Toyota, company President Akio Toyoda said, "We pursued growth over the speed at which we are able to develop people and our organization, and we should sincerely be mindful of that. I regret that this has resulted in the safety issues described in the recalls we face today."

Yet, even as that news was major and breaking all around them, the consultants who brought Lean to the company where I worked—which for the purposes of this book, I will hereon refer to as Woodcutter Enterprises, or WE for short—persisted in emphasizing the Toyota link to Lean. Again, the

Toyota heritage is undeniable and credit is due for not running away from it in times of trouble. But in their constant references to Toyota, the consultants—whose company I will hereafter refer to as Witches and Tyrants Federated, or WTF—seemed totally oblivious to Toyota's troubles. Whenever they mentioned Toyota, it was always in terms that would probably embarrass Toyota's marketing department given the circumstances. We employees at WE were constantly reminded how extremely lucky we were to have our company culture transformed in the likeness of Toyota. Meanwhile, NHTSA was reporting that in response to its fine, Toyota had "agreed to make internal changes to their quality assurance and perform a review of safety-related issues as part of the latest settlement." If decades of being the very embodiment of Lean culture hadn't equipped Toyota with a quality assurance program to save it from a tsunami of fines and recalls, why exactly were we at WE following in its footsteps?

While that obvious question in particular and Toyota's troubles generally were the talk of the water coolers at WE, WTF consultants were demonstrating either utter ignorance or arrogance by not acknowledging any of it. In continuing to anchor what they were doing to our company to *that* company, they were demonstrating that they were either so trapped inside a bubble that they were unaware of Toyota's troubles or they just didn't care to address the elephant in the room with its trunk stuck under the floor mat.

Imagine a coach addressing his team and telling them they will now be adopting the policies and practices of another team, which may have been championship caliber in the past but was currently under suspension for...what have you? Recruiting violations? Gambling? Sexual abuse? Or imagine a general addressing his troops and telling them that they would now be adopting the plans and strategies of the Italian army because...you know...Roman Empire. Every time one of the consultants from WTF held Toyota up as a shining example to us without context or qualification, they undermined not only their own credibility, but also the credibility of the executives at WE who had hired them.

Other Lean practitioners did not share WTF's myopia when it came to Toyota's troubles. Many of the more esteemed members of the Lean fraternity in fact openly wrestled with the dilemma Toyota's plight had created for them on their blogs.

From John Shook, Senior Advisor of the Lean Enterprise Institute:

> "I don't like going into companies and talking on and on about Toyota this and Toyota that ('Toyota is Toyota, we can't BE Toyota, but we can learn from them, etc.'). So, for me 'lean' has always been a convenient way to talk about 'an ideal' that is bigger than just Toyota (though Toyota is our only or best empirical model, so we have to be careful about talking about an 'ideal' that doesn't even exist.) [x]

And Mark Graban, a Lean Shingo Award winning author, wrote:

> "It's disappointing how the mainstream media and the web can't separate Toyota from 'lean manufacturing'...But saying Toyota, the people and the company, failed is not the same as saying lean failed." [xi]

Steven Spear, Lean advocate from MIT, wrote:

"The question was recently posed, did Toyota abandon concern for safety or was safety never part of their culture? With all due respect to the questioner, there are alternative explanations to 'abandon safety' or 'safety never part of their culture.' It is entirely possible (more likely) that safety—both workplace and product—remains part of their culture but maintaining perfection hit bumps in the road." [xii]

And, finally, Professor Jeffrey K. Liker of the University of Michigan wrote:

"The whole environment was set up to find a company to take down, to find a scapegoat and Toyota happened to be that scapegoat." [xiii]

Kudos to all these gentlemen for at least acknowledging Toyota's problems, though I will grant that it might have been easier for them to do so in blogs than it would've been for WTF to do in front of a paying customer. Still there's a bit of the political in each of those responses. Shook, sensing the cock about to crow thrice, tries to distance both Lean and himself from Toyota; Graban takes the old blame-the-media route; Spear attempts to minimize Toyota's failings *vis a vis* its noble and lofty aspirations (much like the politician who famously claimed to have cheated on his multiple wives because he so loved his country). And then Liker, the most heavily invested of all American Lean experts in Toyota's reputation as author of the bestselling *The Toyota Way*, takes the best defense is a good offense approach. Liker went so far as to suggest that Toyota's troubles may have been due to the US government's takeover of General Motors, thus making it the target of a competitor with diabolically enhanced powers. This is the kind of wild speculation more typical of a caller to a radio talk show than an academic who's a self-styled promoter of rational objectivity.

Anyway, even though it does seem as if each of these Lean-men has the makings for a congressional career, the deeper I explored the Lean community's response to Toyota's travails, the more it resembled not the bare-knuckle Cook County style politics of modern American lore, but the ecclesiastic politics of the First Council of Nicaea, 325 AD. As you may recall...or not...that was the early Christian church's first ecumenical gathering convened to settle the Arian controversy, to wit: was Jesus a co-deity with God the Father or was he to inhabit a niche in between—lesser than God but greater than human. In much the same way, the intramural Lean debate seems to swirl around the question: Are Lean and Toyota two in the same God, or is Lean the God and Toyota merely superior to other human organizations?

It's an interesting debate as such inside baseball debates go, though primarily for the amusement of the participants. What I'm afraid the good gentlemen of Lean don't fully comprehend from up in their ivory towers is that for the folks on the factory floor their arcane debate is pretty much meaningless. As a corporate writer, I've had quite a bit of experience with the large gap that exists between those whose jobs take place behind executive doors and those whose jobs take place in more earthy environs, like cubes and factory floors, where one person's pet theory is experienced as other peoples' work day—their job's conditions, compensation, and satisfaction. Except maybe for workers actually dependent on Toyota for their livelihood, the chicken or the egg question as to what came first Toyota or Lean really doesn't matter much. Most workers in possession of their common sense and dignity merely want to know how changes are going to affect their jobs, especially their security...and the more positively the better.

But Lean advocates have been forced to twist themselves into pretzels over this Toyota conundrum because they want it both ways. They want to be able to promise clients and prospects Toyota's purported perfection (according to Spear), its "operational excellence and pristine quality" (according to Liker), its candy covered walls (according to the Brothers Grimm) while at the same time keeping the contract and its escape clause open-ended by invoking continuous improvement—the Lean get out of jail free card. Lean advocates have no one else to blame but themselves for the hit Toyota and in turn Lean have taken in recent years over Toyota's stumbles. They are the ones—with Toyota's oh-so-humble assent—who built Toyota's reputation up beyond reasonable expectations for any human enterprise.

Liker, the most agile of Toyota apologists, was eager to make lemonade out of Toyota's fleet of lemons. Shortly after suggesting that Toyota's problems may have been more due to a media "feeding frenzy," political corruption, and customer stupidity, he wrote:

> "It would be too easy for Toyota to dismiss all of the claims of serious problems as media hype and politically motivated. That would be easy, but not the Toyota way. The Toyota way is to confront problems openly, find the root cause, solve the problems and learn. In the long-term, if [President] Toyoda is successful in leading Toyota to another level of customer responsiveness, we may have an even better model for excellence in the future." [xiv]

There you have it—even when it's bad, Toyota's good. Circling the wagons is an admirable trait, and totally understandable when the wagon train is also your gravy train. I don't want to be too terribly harsh on Liker or others in the Lean community. I certainly don't put them in the same category as the buccaneers

I watched rip my company off under the Lean banner. Through their writings and personal interactions, I have found many Lean practitioners, including the ones I've slighted here, to be sincere in their desire to use tools they dearly believe in to help build better businesses for everyone everywhere. They may, in fact, be sincere to a fault. Their advocacy sometimes borders on zealotry, which introduces a tone of triumphalism into their pronouncements, adding contradiction upon contradiction. After all, a main feature of Lean is supposed to be humility, which really doesn't square with "We're #1" posturing.

In fairness I'll let James Womack, co-founder of LEI, give voice to that humility in this passage he wrote on the Lean/Toyota nexus:

> "Lean methods for product development, fulfillment from order to delivery, supply stream management, customer support, and management of the overall enterprise are now well known and widely accepted in concept. We've won the battle of ideas on how to operate and improve processes. But creating management systems and

organizations that can practice (not just preach) lean every day year after year turns out to be a lot harder. And it's harder for Toyota as well. Many observers have recently noted a gap between the Toyota Production System as an ideal and Toyota's actual production system and between the Toyota Enterprise System as an ideal and Toyota's actual enterprise system, particularly outside of Japan as the company has expanded rapidly across the globe.

"But the wonderful days of Toyota sweeping all before it as it reveals more and more aspects of its value creating methods are done... I now think of Toyota as the big booster rocket that has blasted us out of the slumber of mass production and modern management. But the big booster has done what it can for us and we must be the second stage. It's our task on our watch to put lean in orbit, by which I mean creating sustainable lean enterprises in every industry in every country.

"But we now need to work collaboratively as a group of experimenters from different organizations in a situation where none of us (often including Toyota) knows the best answers to the management and organizational problems we face in the decade ahead. We need to fully share the results of many experiments, decide what doesn't work and (hopefully) what does, and then move on to the next issue." [xv]

Okay, there's a touch of triumphalism there in the beginning, but overall I'd call this about as reasonable and balanced a perspective one could ever hope for out of the messy situation Lean found itself in. There's a clear acknowledgement that the playing field for Lean and Toyota has permanently changed and Lean advocates going forward will not be able to lean on Toyota when making the case for Lean. I've read enough Womack to believe him here. But I think there's a difference between the Lean community that

Womack speaks for and the one represented by firms like WTF. It's a bit like the difference between family farming and factory farming—the one is truly close to the ground and has a stake in the product of its labors; the other is big, artificial and fully vested in its own profit margin. WTF will ride the Toyota-built bandwagon as long as gullible clients and prospects allow it to, or until someone pulls back the curtain. So—without further ado—let's see what's behind the curtain.

WIZARD OF OZ

"Hush, my dear," he said. "Don't speak so loud, or you will be overheard—and I should be ruined. I'm supposed to be a Great Wizard."

"And aren't you?" she asked.

"Not a bit of it, my dear; I'm just a common man."

"You're less than that," said the Scarecrow, in a grieved tone. "You're a humbug."

"Exactly so!" declared the little man, rubbing his hands together as if it pleased him. "I am a humbug."

"But this is terrible," said the Tin Woodman. "How shall I ever get my heart?"

"Or I my courage?" asked the Lion.

"Or I my brains?" wailed the Scarecrow, wiping the tears from his eyes with his coat sleeve.

"My dear friends," said Oz, "I pray you not to speak of these little things. Think of me, and the terrible trouble I'm in at being found out."

"Doesn't anyone else know you're a humbug?" asked Dorothy.

"No one knows it but you—and myself," replied Oz.

In *The Wizard of Oz*, when Dorothy first enters the throne room of the Emerald City, she is greeted by a large, disembodied head that bellows at her in a deep, powerful voice, "I am Oz, the Great and Terrible. Who are you, and why do you seek me?" She replies, "I am Dorothy, the Small and Meek. I have come to you for help."

The scene that transpired at my company, Woodcutter Enterprises, when employees were first ushered into a large assembly room for our orientation to Lean wasn't exactly like Dorothy's meeting with the Wizard, but that was much the essence of it. Small and meek may be overstating it a bit, but I'd say anxiety was definitely in the air. A few years prior, like many companies in late 2008, we were hit with significant layoffs. The sight of co-workers trudging off to HR to get the bad news and trudging back with severance packages in their hands and shock or tears in their eyes had made an indelible impression as the most disturbing sight in our company's recent history. The American economy was hardly doing much better since that day, so the idea that something called Lean was about to make a presence at the company sent a cold wind through our resplendent Southern California location.

Our company president must have anticipated the anxiety because she sought to alleviate it at the outset by assuring us all that no jobs would be lost as a result of our Lean transformation. Discerning minds, however, immediately had to wonder how an all out effort to eliminate waste, as the Lean process was billed, could avoid finding waste in staffing. Sheer logic dictated that if the company had detected enough waste of time and resources to invest as heavily as it was about to in Lean, there had to be an inkling at least that some waste in manpower would also be found. Our president met that unspoken concern by assuring us further that any redundancy or waste Lean revealed in staffing would be met by the company's commitment to place affected employees into areas the Lean process revealed needed help. It would, in other words, be like unicorns or like the magic Washington lawmakers try to conjure up when they talk of reducing the national debt by closing tax loopholes. Everyone so very much wants to believe.

This was no time for skepticism; our company was on the brink of an exciting new adventure--or something like that. And I certainly wasn't the one to entertain doubts about it. I had previously become familiar with Lean through a good friend who had been teaching, writing, and practicing Lean for much of a decade, and I had heard his firsthand and rather convincing stories of Lean success. So I joined my co-workers in extending our guest every courtesy as he made a PowerPoint presentation that would help orient us all for the big and important process that was about to transform our daily work lives for the foreseeable future.

As a foreshadowing of what was to come, the presentation began with Toyota...lots and lots about Toyota...all the way back to its days as a loom maker. (Similar to what was said about the campaign speeches of a famous politician, much of our presenter's spiel seemed to consist of a noun, a verb, and *Toyota!*) For the purposes of this book, I will call our presenter Prof. Marvel after the character in *The Wizard of Oz.* Like the character in the movie, he was what might be called a roly-poly fellow. I don't believe people should ever have their physicality held against them. It's at best unprofessional and at worst cruel. But the juxtaposition of a program called Lean with a

Lean spokesman whose belly hangs over his belt was a little disorienting—a bit like being greeted at Hooters by a flat-chested hostess. Bad, unprofessional thoughts, however, became practically unavoidable when Prof. Marvel himself drew attention to the incongruity. He told us that the Lean techniques we were about to learn were so solid that we would be able to apply them in our personal lives just as he had done, he said, in his ongoing efforts to lose weight. Then he smiled in that way public speakers do when they want to let us know they're one of us and added, "Well, you can see it hasn't done me much good." Indeed.

Before that daring bit of self-deprecation could arouse even a hint of nervous laughter, he launched into an hour-long non-sequitur in which he proceeded to tell us that despite the fact that Lean could not help him eliminate waste from his own body, it would lean up our company of over a thousand employees scattered all over globe. It was a rather breathtaking display of whatever is the opposite of humility.

I would learn subsequently that the connection between personal diet and Lean business transformations was not unique to our presenter. I've seen it show up a number of times in my research for this book. Here's a passage from a blogger trying to explain away Lean's dismal success rate:

> "Implementing lean is like taking regular exercise. It isn't easy but done right it can benefit anybody. My own abysmal failure to maintain an exercise regime does not change this.
>
> "Exceptional athletes have the dedication to take their exercise and training all the way to Olympic gold. Their achievements do not make the rest of us failures, their achievements inspire us all to try harder." [xvi]

First off, I've never met anyone inspired to lose weight by Olympic athletes...an upcoming high school reunion maybe...a favorite dress that no longer fits, perhaps. But *I want a body like Michael Phelps*? I don't think so. And I do hate to be taking these things so literally, but I'm by trade a writer and editor and do believe that if Lean practitioners were as meticulous about words as they are about numbers, they would improve their overall credibility substantially. But I digress.

There are two much larger points in the passage. One is that it pretty much affirms rather than refutes Lean's failure rate, contrary to the blogger's intent. After all, the number of human beings that succeed at becoming Olympic athletes probably coordinates better with the number of companies that succeed at becoming Lean than those that don't.

Two is that this reference to the personal failings of dieters is not so much to strike a note of humility, as it is to raise a question of character. The implication is that if you fail in your commitment to Lean it is due to the same character flaw that accounts for your inability to lose weight. It is a scolding message that would be echoed throughout our company's Lean transformation and is a stroke of quite insidious genius.

Anyway, the presentation was not only at odds with its presenter but with itself. During the course of it, Prof. Marvel extolled the virtue of Thomas Edison's legendary stick-to-itiveness, repeating the well-worn story of Edison's doggedness in the face of failed experiments that's been a staple of business speakers since the Wizard of Menlo Park declared that genius was 90% perspiration. Yet, in direct contrast, the portrait of the coming Lean paradise our presenter painted for us would not have allowed for either Edison's genius or his perspiration. It was, we were told, a process that would flow by constant, methodical elimination of error. For example, we were told, if Coca Cola had been a Lean company in 1985, it would've saved itself the embarrassing failure of New Coke by requiring as part of its process a market test of the product. This observation was followed by another whiplash segue into Steve Jobs's visionary leadership of Apple. It was left for those of us in the audience who knew somewhat more about Jobs than we had about Toyota's loom heritage to figure out what Jobs had to do with Lean. Among his other notable non-Lean-like attributes, Jobs was famously against test marketing and believed in creating products consumers did not yet know they wanted.

But Jobs is destined to loom over the next century as the reigning business icon, as Edison loomed over the last. So no matter how irrelevant his genius may be to whatever methodology is being sold at the moment, hearing his name dropped, as it was with Edison's, is something business audiences will have to get used to for the next hundred years because name dropping (like *Toyota!*) is a prime tool of the consultant's trade, Lean or not.

There were two slides in Prof. Marvel's presentation that particularly stood out. The first portrayed a medieval military commander armed only with a sword who is so obsessed with the battle in front of him that he brushes away some very innovative fellow who's brought him a Gatling gun. Aside from being ahistorical (medieval war? Gatling gun? Well, hey, it's a cartoon...so whatever), the cartoon was counterproductive. A farmer struggling with a horse and plow while someone tries to sell him a tractor or a secretary working at a typewriter while someone attempts to sell her a computer could've more positively gotten the message across that we sometimes get so stuck doing things the way we've always done them that we overlook new, improved ways of doing them. A better choice also would've eliminated the war and slaughter imagery from a presentation to an audience you've already acknowledged was on edge about people getting terminated.

The second unforgettable slide was worse—and not just from the standpoint of breaking the first rule of PowerPoint by jamming so much information on one slide that it should've come with a label warning that swallowing it whole could cause choking. I'd like to reproduce the slide here for full appreciation, but it's proprietary, and I do want to honor that. So let me just limit myself to this: *Elizabeth Kübler-Ross*. Yes, there prominently displayed on the slide was the name of Kübler-Ross, who is known for one thing and one thing only: delineating the five stages of grief. And there on the slide were two of her stages: denial and anger in largely incomprehensible context. Why? What did it mean? Hard to tell. It would've taken a wizard to tell, but the only wizard around was Prof. Marvel and he wasn't saying. This slide deserves special mention here because, first, it captured the glut of information that came our way that day. A daylong presentation could've been built around this slide alone. More importantly the slide deserves to be highlighted because in some vague, inchoate way it dealt with the question of morale. Shockingly, that would be an issue that WTF failed to address as its Lean process unfolded, driving down our company morale and ultimately inspiring this book.

Along the way—as happened on the road to Oz—we came upon a poppy field and a lot of people just fell asleep. For those few of us who were able to stay awake through Prof. Marvel's soporific presentation, however, visions of winged monkeys appeared on the horizon. As a good and loyal employee I tried to sound a warning. Immediately after the presentation, I went to my computer and sent a memo to my superiors detailing how uninspiring and incomprehensible it had been. I raised the issues of contradiction and incoherence I've raised here, and I also questioned the presentation's operating metaphor, which the speaker said was "a shower." Some things, he said, would stick and some things would not. As a writer, I believe we're all entitled to our own metaphors, and as it turns out this was a pretty accurate one because the presentation really was like a shower. As I told my superiors in my memo, the water in a shower doesn't stick. It bounces off or gets dried off. Better to have said he was just throwing spaghetti at the wall—or us. At least with spaghetti there would be a reasonable expectation of something sticking.

It is indicative of the kind of company ours was at the time that the two top executives I addressed my memo to were both receptive to it. They expressed appreciation for my views and engaged me in open and direct discussion about those views without a hint of hostility or defensiveness. The entire exchange was marked by a mutual respect, which I believed had been and would continue to be a key aspect of our company's culture. I felt good about speaking up when and as I did, and truly felt it would have a positive impact on our Lean rollout.

So it was more than a little dismaying when two months later WE hired Prof. Marvel away from WTF to lead our Lean transformation from the inside. I have learned since that it is not uncommon for this kind of transaction where consultants sell the client on the need to place experts just like them in-house in order to achieve the goal of the consulting mission. Who better positioned to get that work than the person you bring in from the outside to tell you what you need? (And that shadow following your new employee through the door is called conflict of interest.)

In the intervening months, Prof. Marvel—now Vice President Marvel—did nothing to boost his standing among staff and alleviate the widespread bafflement at his sudden ascension. The first impression he had created at the orientation had taken hold (except, it seems, with the only people that mattered, the powers that be). As our Lean transformation unfolded over time, that poor first impression, both of the presenter and the message, would resonate with sorry consequences. At the risk of getting ahead of my narrative, I should note in hindsight some of the other humbuggery in that first presentation because it became the mortar for the monument to corporate hypocrisy WTF would help WE build on the foundation of its 80-year commitment to credibility.

In one of the early slides in the presentation we were told that it takes time to change processes and cultures. The mission to change our company's culture was repeated over and over again, almost as many times as we were told what a great culture we *already* had at WE...which echoed what we had been told for years by our leaders...and our industry at large. At no point did anyone in WTF (or frankly from our company leadership) feel at all compelled to either address this contradiction or to tell staff what it was in the existing culture that had to be changed. Or more importantly—as would turn out—what the change we were going to try and achieve would look like.

In the very same slide, we were told that whatever this change was it wouldn't be easy, and in fact would be painful for some. "Change is hard" became a mantra among the missionaries from WTF and its acolytes among our own staff. It became the go-to conversation stopper when skeptical questions were raised about the unfolding process. More annoying and insulting was the way the people guiding us through this process delivered the line as if it were revealed wisdom that might some day be within our grasp if only we could manage our pain well enough to change.

The entire process, another slide claimed, would be based first and foremost on respect for people. Although this sentiment was echoed through subsequent slides and in every piece of media material WTF put before us, it was contradicted by statements, activities, events, corporate directives, and individual behaviors that clearly established process, not people, as king. WTF inundated the company with charts and methodologies, which relegated people to moveable objects on a magnetized whiteboard.

A series of slides dealt with "8 Wastes." Among these wastes were wasted motion and wasted human talent. As the Lean transformation progressed, the company was dogged by troubling ergonomics issues brought on by WTF's ideas about workflow. Furthermore, despite the excruciating effort put into creating colorful, ubiquitous workflow charts, critical crunch periods would find key personnel sitting idle while others were forced to work overtime.

Another slide addressed the problem of "overburden," which the slide informed us was caused by failure to engage staff and created stress by asking too much in too little time. Within months of launching our Lean transformation, the stress level throughout the company was palpable. Much of it was due to the pressure put on managers to participate in a seemingly nonstop series of Rapid Improvement Events, or RIEs, which consumed most of their work days and weeks and left many employees disengaged at best and adrift at worst.

There was a series of slides that...what's the verb I need here? Yes, a series of slides that showered down on us a hailstorm of acronyms and terms with little or no explanation. The same terms would reappear again and again throughout the transformation with no regard to whether any of this part of the shower was sticking—A3, 6S, true North metrics, VSA, pull, takt time, standard of work. An orientation is always going to be somewhat disorienting in this regard because you're introducing new terminology to an audience. What was maddening about this presentation was the shower metaphor that drove it and would actually drive the entire WTF approach. There not only was little attempt to teach, there didn't seem to be any real concern about teaching at anything other than the most superficial and indifferent level.

The almost willful effort to mystify rather than clarify seemed to dovetail nicely with WTF's frequent reminders of what a long, arduous process we had undertaken (5 years long per its contract). And thus another element of hypocrisy was introduced in that orientation that would play out through the transformation, which was how very un-lean WTF was in its own processes. They were redundant, protracted, unfocused, and seemed to be trying to make up in quantity what they lacked in quality.

The scene from *The Wizard of Oz* highlighted at the beginning of this chapter takes place just after Toto, Dorothy's dog, exposes the wizard for the humbug he is. What harm WTF did to WE might not have been so egregious if the representatives it sent into our company presented themselves as ordinary men (and note, they were all men). But they tried to present themselves as something much more than that, and therein lay the real humbug.

BIBBIDI-BOBBIDI-BOO

*Salagadoola mechicka boola bibbidi-bobbidi-boo
Put 'em together and what have you got
bibbidi-bobbidi-boo
Salagadoola mechicka boola bibbidi-bobbidi-boo
It'll do magic believe it or not
bibbidi-bobbidi-boo
Salagadoola means mechicka booleroo
But the thingmabob that does the job is
bibbidi-bobbidi-boo*

Like Cinderella's bibbidi-bobbidi-boo, we were introduced to a magic word that might help speed us through the drudgery of our work fast enough to get us to the ball on time—or wherever it was we were heading. The word was *sensei,* a Japanese word for teacher—fortunately a humbler choice than wizard. Still, the word played right into the aura of Japan as insinuated into the thinking of a generation raised on *Karate Kid* movies. A *sensei* could be our Mister Miyagi, and WE could be the grasshopper.

Miyagi: We make sacred pact. I promise teach karate to you. You promise learn. I say. You do. No questions.

And that bit of movie dialog right there pretty much sums up how things went wrong right from the start. Our people from top to bottom went into the relationship with WTF accepting a subordinate position...accepting that the men coming into our company at an elevated and esteemed position were worthy of it. In effect, our leadership trusted their leadership to provide us with qualified personnel to guide us through one of the most expensive and extensive changes in our company's history. This happens all the time of course when you hire, say, a construction outfit to build an extension to your headquarters or an IT team to build a website for you. You don't get to do the hiring or even review the employees of the outside contractor you hire to complete these tasks. But nor do you accept at face value the infallible wisdom of the people the contractor sends in to do the job, nor—more importantly—do you force your people to accept the judgment of their people as to how best to do jobs your people have been doing for years and their people have never done. Yet, that was the dynamic created once we had to accept that the men now guiding our company's future were to be regarded at as considerably more than what they were—which was vendors.

Sensei was only the first of many Japanese words that would be put forth as part of our new company culture. Another one was *hansei*—a rather good word actually. It means to acknowledge your own mistake upon deep personal reflection and to pledge improvement. I approve of that concept and wish American business executives displayed more of it. US corporate heads are more likely to make public apology after deep reflection with the corporate attorney and corporate PR department than any deep personal reflection. Though I should mention here that at the end of the first Lean event I participated in, our company president did in fact engage in an act of *hansei*, though neither I nor most others in the room knew the word at the time. She told us how midway through the initial Lean training she and our other top people went through prior to introducing it to staff, she had serious doubts about whether Lean would be right for WE. When she expressed her reservations to her counterpart from WTF, she said, he looked her straight in the eye and told her that her company had suffered in 2008, and it was time for her to accept responsibility for that.

> *Miyagi*: We make sacred pact. I promise
> teach karate to you. You promise learn. I
> say. You do. No questions.

It was a remarkable show of corporate humility, and I made a point of immediately complimenting our president on it. But like so much that would be said and promised and planned and envisioned during these Lean events, it didn't hold up well on second thought. It's not that our president's sincerity was in question, but her self-regard. In submitting to that line of intimidation, she was both inflating her role in the 2008 global economic meltdown and selling herself short for actions she took—pre-Lean—to cushion the company from even harder consequences. As Daniel Kahneman writes, company heads get too much credit when things go well and too much blame when they don't, and not many executives anywhere outside of the giants of the US financial industry could've done much to avert what happened in 2008. But before it happened our president had made a couple of decisions to expand the company into the right places at the right time, and those decisions would be significant in helping the company recover sooner than most.

So, why'd she do it? Why did she give in to such rank guilt-tripping? Well, in-depth psychoanalysis can always be helpful in answering these questions. But off the top, I'd say this is the inevitable outcome of giving someone a dominant role in a relationship as a matter of form. Future instances of such compliance by others in our leadership would suggest an overall submission to the role of grasshopper. This posture is commendable to a degree. We really would be better off if our leaders acted like learners more often. But the entire concept is so indicative of the considerable cultural clash between Japan and the US. In their culture, it's not unusual for a failed executive to commit *hari-kari*; in ours it's more typical for a failed executive to receive a golden parachute. In theirs, workers are more inclined to surrender their autonomy to authority; in ours, workers place a higher premium on individualism. Much of the success of Lean in Japan is due specifically to the culture of the Japanese.

Lean advocates believe they can accommodate our culture to theirs by the wholesale importation of Japanese words for application to US Lean transformations. In addition to *sensei* and *hansei*, those words include, among many others, *Yoketen*, *kaniban*, *kaizen*, *muda*, *mura*, and *muri*. Muri's another good one, meaning unreasonableness or absurdity. And speaking of absurdity, there's *hanedashi*, which according to WTF's official glossary means *"Device or means of automatic unload of the work piece from one operation or process, providing the proper state for the next work piece to be loaded. Automatic unloading and orientation for the next process is essential for a Chaku-Chaku line."*

What, you say? Don't know *Chaku-Chaku*? It means Load-Load, Reader-san.

As you may have noticed, aside from being Japanese, the usage there is primarily for a factory setting, as is most of the Lean vocabulary, Japanese or not. This is only natural, since the whole movement spent 50 years marinating in the factory environment until alchemists like WTF came along to expand its reach. As a result, they spend a great deal of time trying to shoehorn factory-related words and concepts into Information Age environments where those of us sitting at computers have very little use or comprehension of unloading one piece of work before loading another piece.

But rather than let a Lean language emerge out of the experimentation to find a new identity for Lean in a new non-Toyota environment as James Womack has suggested, a cut and paste outfit like WTF simply chooses to recycle hand-me-downs from Japanese factory workers to American office workers. They do this partially, I suspect, because it's easy. But I also think they do it because it helps perpetuate their mystique. The more complex the mere language is for us to grasp, the more it seems we need interpreters...or, as it were, *senseis*.

One of the most annoying of these words and a good one for illustrating what's wrong with this process is *gemba*. The WTF glossary says that in Japan it literally means "real place." They take that literal definition and stretch it to mean a walk to where the "real" work is done. An American manager without benefit of Lean might simply say, "I think I'll go walk the floor." Or maybe, if he or she is a person of few words, "Let's go for a walk." But in Lean, it can't be just a walk; it has to a *gemba* walk. Even that would not be so pretentious in a factory environment where you could actually watch machine operators operate or conveyor belts convey. In an office full of computers, however, there is limited action on those monitors. Our company's *gemba* walkers made a game try of it in the beginning, walking into cubes and offices unannounced and standing over people's shoulders as they cut video together or composed scripts. After a very short while that irritation passed and was replaced by chart watching. As a result of Lean, our work areas proliferated with charts, which took on immense significance as the keys to our ultimate transformation. Thus our workdays would regularly be interrupted as troops of *gemba* walkers marched into our work areas and discussed the make-up and progress of these charts. For 20 minutes or more, 6-8 people would gather around these charts conducting standing meetings that in a factory would mercifully be drowned out by the sound of machinery. In an office environment, the *gemba* walks became the noise in the machine.

After a while these exercises took on the appearance of sheer exhibitionism. It was, "Hey, everybody, look at us. We're on a *gemba* walk!" Suspicions began to grow that the *gemba* walks, like the proliferation of charts and Post-it's all around our complex, were part of WTF's attempt to establish its presence, put its brand on us. It surely could not have been part of the Lean ideal to have all these people walking from one location in the company to another to stand around interrupting the work of so many others when all they had to do was call up a digital copy of a chart and discuss it in the quiet and comfort of a meeting room...or, rather, as a Lean meeting room would come to be called, an *obeya*.

I'm not making a stand for jingoism here. Certainly one of the great strengths of the US is its diversity, which not only welcomes people from other lands, but vocabulary from other lands. Thus we're comfortable with *habeas corpus* in our Constitution; *terracotta* on our roofs; *sommelier, salsa*, and *sushi* in our restaurants. No one minds a touch of the foreign. It's exotic and broadening in moderation. Lean overdoes it to the detriment of those trying to go Lean as well as those trying to take them there. Despite what the old pop song says, we are not turning Japanese and not likely to any time soon. The novelty of these words wears off after about a month, and the imposition of them sets the stage for trouble down the road. Months into a Lean transformation when managers and staff start getting disenchanted with it, the Japanese lingo provides an easy target for mockery as well as a key to the door of detachment.

It's not just the surfeit of Japanese words that's a problem. As with so many pseudo-technical undertakings, Lean also feels compelled to show off the usual assortment of acronyms, jargon, and run of the mill mumbo jumbo. Behold this list from WTF's working vocabulary:

- CEDAC—Cause and Effect Diagram with the Addition of Cards
- PDCA—Plan-Do-Check-Act
- Takt—derived from the German for cycle time
- TTA--takt time attainment
- SWIP—Standard Work in Progress
- Race to the Red
- CI--continuous improvement
- Kaizen—planned and structured process improvement
- SQDIP—Safety, Quality, Delivery, Inventory, Production

- Standard Work
- VOC—Voice of the customer
- VS—Value Stream
- VSA—Value Stream Analysis
- MDI—Metric for Daily Improvement
- NVA—Non Value Added
- JiT—Just in Time
- Flow
- Flow Cells
- RIE—Rapid Improvement Events
- AHP—Analytic Hierarchy Process
- Gap analysis
- X-Metric
- Sprint
- 6S

Those terms would be layered on top of the vocabulary particular to any company, and our company had plenty enough of its own lingo. WTF promoted its arcane glossary on the grounds that it would give everyone in the company a common language with which to go through our Lean transformation. I don't know how extensively other companies buy into that line of thinking, but I did get to visit a company where the Lean implementation seemed to be working (a tour I'll discuss later in this book). That company made a point of customizing all the Lean language to facilitate its employees' ease of comprehension. In other words—and I do mean other words—when they established a process to get at root causes, they simply called the process *The AJAX Company's Problem Solving Metric*...no faux tech sounding gobbledygook...no Japanese imports.

This common sense approach might have reduced WTF's vaunted 6S process to what it was known as before their expertise arrived on the scene, namely spring-cleaning. In years past, HR would send out a memo designating a day or more for spring-cleaning. We maybe didn't do it as often as we should have, or as deep as 6S demanded. But then again, our simple spring-cleaning never produced the antagonism that WTF did in forcing us to do it their way.

Ironically with so much concern about imposing a common language on all of us, WTF's efforts at our company were plagued by miscommunication, even around something as simple-minded as 6S. As I say, 6S is your basic spring-cleaning complicated by a factor of 6:

1. Sort
2. Straighten
3. Scrub
4. Safety
5. Standardize
6. Sustain

As soon as the first 6S in our building was completed, rumors started flying that WTF was going to require us to place color tape on our desks to outline distinct areas for each of our desk items. Desks suddenly appeared with taped areas designated-- rectangular for stapler, square for phone, circular for coffee cup. We would also be limited to three personal items per work area. The reaction against this among staff yet to do a 6S was swift and emotional. Our WE Lean team quickly tried to back-pedal. Taping off desk areas was strictly voluntary, they claimed. It would just be for those of us who needed help organizing our desks--and knowing where to find our phones presumably. As for the three personal items per workstation, we were told, this was now under review and a committee would be formed to determine exactly how many and what kind of personal items would be allowed.

This flare-up added an air of hostility when my particular department was called in for its pre-6S orientation. When we were told about the committee that would determine how many personal objects would eventually be allowed in our work areas, we asked who would make up this committee and what criteria they would follow. The answer was that those things had not yet been determined, but they were not matters for us to worry about. When this *sensei* (who I will call Señor Wences—"S'alright? S'alright!") took us through a 6S slide presentation and asked us what "sort" meant and what "straighten" meant and what "scrub" meant, to a man and woman we refused to act like sixth graders. No one responded. When he showed us a slide of a tool cabinet with its doors off and told us that WTF wants us to take doors off cabinets and closets to facilitate what it calls "visual management," it took us as a group less than a minute to raise obvious objections. "What about stored valuables?" asked one of my co-workers. "What about stored toxins?" asked another. "What about earthquakes?" asked a third.

"Well," Señor Wences answered, less than sagely, "You can replace them with see-through plexiglass doors."

During the 6S itself, this cavalier response to any resistance we raised to throwing certain things out reached a contentious stage. When members of our department protested against tossing items out for fear of needing them in the future, Señor Wences would forcefully invoke the Lean principle of eliminating waste as defined as anything of no immediate use. When he was asked what if we had unseen future uses, he would tell us that we could buy replacements.

WTF was generous in giving lip service to the Socratic ideal of asking questions, but the catch seemed to be that employees could ask why of themselves, but not why of WTF. A few days after our 6S, two members of our department--loyal employees of nearly 50 years combined service--were summoned to HR and told in no uncertain terms that they were to get with the program without further complaint because the process the company was now undergoing would not tolerate "antibodies." Antibody was the exact word used—without irony, embarrassment, or seeming understanding of the meaning of the word as a necessity for a body to successfully fight off invading viruses.

A few months later a call went out for a large retail set that had been constructed for our company's educational filming. Word came back that the set had been thrown out during the 6S because it hadn't been used in 6 years. A new set would have to be built. WTF seemed to make a curious distinction between wastefulness when it came to company resources and furnishing and wastefulness when it came to company funds. Whether this distinction was spelled out when WE negotiated its contract with WTF is a matter for bookkeepers to decide. All I can say is that the view from the factory floor suggested that WTF could make WE's money disappear quicker than you could say *Bibbidi-bobbidi-boo.*

MAGIC BEANS

"It's lucky I met you," said the butcher. "You may save yourself the trouble of going so far." With this, he put his hand in his pocket, and pulled out five curious-looking beans. "What do you call these?" he asked Jack.

"Beans," answered Jack.

"Yes," said the butcher. "Beans, but they're the most wonderful beans that ever were known. If you plant them overnight, by the next morning they'll grow up and reach the sky. And to save you the trouble of going all the way to market, I don't mind exchanging them for that cow of yours."

"Done!" cried Jack, who was so delighted with the bargain that he ran all the way home to tell his mother how lucky he had been.

Let it not be said that WTF came to the grand party WE insisted on throwing for it empty-handed. Its bag was chock full of beans that, if not exactly magic, would create for our executives at least the illusion that one day a giant beanstalk would sprout in our parking lot and rise upward into the sky where a pot of corporate gold would be waiting—ours for the taking.

Speaking of that parking lot, the first visible sign to staff that WTF was coming was when we received notice that there would no longer be executive parking spaces...that, in the democratizing spirit of Lean, all parking spots would be equal. This fanfare for the common man was echoed when the first RIEs began to roll out, and we were told that a key feature of them would be that "titles are left at the door." Inside the RIE all men and women, like parking spots, would be created equal.

In both instances, the implied nobility was undeniable. But as I've said before, much put forth by WTF did not hold up well to closer scrutiny. The first-come, first-serve parking directive struck many employees as trivial. The assigned executive spaces opened up by the new policy did not positively impact enough spaces or distance to make it at all recognizable as a benefit to employees. Nor were employees in any measurable number begrudging executives who had earned their reserved spots through their positions and needed those spots due to their often busy travel schedules.

Employees instinctively understand their place, even those employees who believe they deserve a higher place...or don't like the people in higher places. If you're going to try to undo centuries of employee conditioning to obey the hierarchy, at least put some effort into it. Perhaps it would have been useful to devote some pre-RIE time to exploring what "leaving titles at the door" means in practical terms. What fears would both employees and managers feel operating in such an environment? What would it take for management to prove that it was really willing and able to operate in such an environment without consequences for the employee? And what about this new, alien and intimidating title that had just been introduced to us—*sensei*? Does that title get left at the door? Can the *sensei's* authority be challenged, as well?

The very idea that you might break down this fundamental aspect of corporate culture with a mere announcement of "Please leave titles at the door" was naïve at best and willfully deceptive at worst. Because over time I came to believe the worst of WTF, I'm inclined to believe that deception was the intent...and deception not just aimed at staff to make them believe that for the hours spent in RIEs their bosses were really their peers, but deception aimed at the executives as well, to keep them humbled in the presence *not* of their staff, but the *sensei*.

If these democratizing gestures had been reinforced and expanded through the course of our Lean transformation, I may very well have come to a more favorable conclusion about WTF's intent. But quite the opposite happened as WTF increasingly warned against dissenting voices—"change the people or *change the people*" entered our company lexicon for the first time—and the democratic trappings proved to be a sham.

By the second year of our Lean transformation, "trust the process" had replaced "change is hard" as the all-purpose conversation stopper and answer to any difficult question. The "process" seemingly was a shape-shifting creature of myriad appendages and faculties. Its constant movement and metamorphoses made it difficult enough to track let alone trust.

Among them were the RIEs of mostly 5-days' duration with detailed plans for each day, Thursdays being the most ambitious:

- View and record operative conditions
- Troubleshoot solutions to problems identified on day 1-3
- Begin applying solutions
- Identify action plan to take place within 30 days of RIE
- Determine ways to sustain solutions
- Validate process alterations
- Create sketches and slide presentation to summarize week's work for Friday Report Out

Then there was A3 thinking, the process of getting all your thinking down on one piece of metric-sized paper called an A3, similar to an 11" x 17" piece of paper (which raises the question for all those *let's go Japanese* Leaniacs out there: how's that metric system translating to the USA?) The A3 is divided into 9 steps:

1. State the problem
2. Measure the initial state
3. Set the target state
4. Find the root cause
5. Develop a solution
6. Test the hypothesis
7. Create the plan

8. Track the benefits
9. Share the knowledge

The A3, we were told, should capture the logic of solving a problem on a single sheet and be able to stand on its own without explanation. Nowhere in the known universe has so much thinking been contained on one piece of paper since the death of Einstein.

Then early in year two the X-Matrix appeared. Our WE Lean leadership spent a week in an RIE with a *sensei* learning its seeming *light saber*-like powers. When our leaders emerged for their report out, they could tell us how hard the X-Matrix had been to master and how wonderful it was once you did, but they could not explain it to staff and admitted as much. Also, they couldn't adequately demonstrate its usefulness to us...or in Lean terminology: WIIFM (what's in it for me).

After X-Matrix came POP (and SNAP and CRACKLE and PRESTO and SHAZAAM, or some such words, all designed to conjure up the illusion of speed and alacrity). In between, Standard of Work reared its ugly little head. This is what WTF prescribed as "typical standard work elements":

- Daily track area managers' standard work

- Daily track takt attainment of all value streams
- Daily gemba walk with operations managers
- Daily 6S audit—one area per day, randomly & in rotation—follow-up on issues raised in last audit
- Daily monitor standard of work of all team members—area manager, team leader, lead, operator—randomly and in rotation
- Weekly gemba walk with multiple team leaders
- Weekly assess metrics for MDI

Oh, yes, almost forgot: MDI—Metric for Daily Improvement. Somewhere along the line if you had been cursed with a management position you would have created an MDI board with your daily improvement metrics spelled out in particulate detail.

And WTF would not tolerate slackers, warning our top people:

- Leaders at the top must be disciplined in their dedication to the lean process to make it work
- Leaders below the top level must be equally disciplined
- Leaders who disregard abnormal situations make them normal

- Leaders who fail in their dedication will fail to create an effective lean culture
- Leaders must demand standard work from all staff without exception
- Leaders must set the standard

Well, one person's discipline is another person's anality. I'm rather happy to report that in a year-and-a-half I never saw one of our leaders adhere to that standard of work...not even come close. I really do look upon this as a good thing. The atmosphere WTF managed to create at our company was oppressive enough without having top executives wander through the work areas on a regular basis checking to see how well we were all doing at sorting, straightening and scrubbing our workstations. And even if our top people didn't have the good sense to ignore most of the anal retentive aspects of the Lean process, the nonstop carousel of RIEs they were required to attend made it impossible to perform their standard of work to WTF's specifications.

I don't want to come off as some kind of troglodyte here. I'm all for change that makes life and work better. For years I started my writing projects...or any complex project...with a legal pad. I'd outline what I wanted to write about or make columns for pros and cons and deadlines on whatever other project I was about to undertake. I also started each and every day with a Post-it of my "things to do." But then along came writers' software to help with my outlines; "thinking" software to help with brainstorming, organizing, and charting; and a smartphone to replace my need for Post-it notes with both writing and vocal functionality. Lean's affinity for Post-its and wall charts is quaint at best, but at worst it is that highest of Lean crimes: wasteful. For months on end we watched as long strips of butcher paper lined our company walls to become populated with different color Post-its with hand scribbled ideas, directions, insights, and answers to questions no one but WTF ever thought to ask...or needed to ask. The strips would later be photographed and carefully moved room to room to be transcribed for reports and archived, leaving those of us working in the Information Age rather than the Industrial Age to wonder: Hasn't anybody here heard of digitizing? Web connecting? Mobile devices?

The reliance on Post-its and handmade charts seems more a matter of Lean branding than Lean efficiency. These are artifacts passed on from Lean's roots in factory settings where computerized tools were nonexistent. Lean practitioners, or at least WTF, appear reluctant to modernize their practices for fear of losing their Lean identity even as they attempt to modernize their portfolios with more Information Age clients.

But this isn't just a matter of style. In fact there are more serious issues of substance. On the matter of A3 thinking, for instance, I would argue that the A3 is much more a tool for organizing thinking than thinking itself. It really isn't much different than a simple pluses and minuses sheet, except it asks for more product or detail from your thinking. For getting at the actual thinking process, it is immaterial.

We are on the new frontier of neuroscience. This discipline abounds with data as to *how* we think—or, as they say, what makes us tick. There is enough information out there in the early stages of neuroscience to tell us how certain people are likely to fill out an A3, which people are likely to make the most use of an A3, which the least likely.

Daniel Kahneman breaks our thinking process down into two types—fast and slow. Fast is what psychologists call System 1; slow is what they call System 2. Writes Kahneman:

> "When we think of ourselves, we identify with System 2, the conscious, reasoning self that has beliefs, makes choices, and decides what to think about and what to do. Although System 2 believes itself to be where the action is, the automatic System 1 is the hero...effortlessly originating impressions and feelings that are the main source of the explicit beliefs and deliberate choices of System 2. The automatic operations of System 1 generate surprisingly complex patterns of ideas, but only the slower System 2 can construct thoughts in an orderly series of steps." [xvii]

I am all for that System 2 construction of thoughts into orderly steps. And I truly believe that is a genuine plus of what its proponents like to call Lean thinking. And I'm happy to report that I saw an example of this process in practice when I was on that Lean tour I mentioned earlier. At one of the companies on the tour, we were shown their proprietary problem-solving matrix, which they used to get at the root cause of a bottleneck in accounts receivable. On completion, the matrix revealed that the conventional wisdom that held that the company's credit department was the source of the bottleneck was wrong. The credit department played a minor role compared to two other departments, which were largely responsible for the bottleneck. And in the best of Lean fashion, these results led to fixing the problem, rather than fixing blame.

In fairness, through its efforts WTF actually had a few qualitative breakthroughs like this at WE. Unfortunately these quality wins were buried under an avalanche of quantitative data. Rather than taking the few, small victories and leveraging them throughout the company in a way designed to show employees what was in it for them, WTF chose to trumpet its vast collection of numbers...how much staff put through how many RIEs in how little time; how many tons of material discarded during 6S; how many new tools introduced to company leadership. This is because WTF wasn't so much interested in what was in it for us, the employees, but rather what was in it for them as a major purveyor of enterprise-wide Lean transformations. Small wins suited neither their corporate strategy nor their corporate ego.

From the factory floor, watching our management operate in a constant state of discombobulation was most damaging to our entire Lean transformation. Our leaders didn't so much get a tool chest opened up to them as they had it dumped on their heads. One top-level person—and one of our company's savviest—confided to me one day that even though he (or she) had participated in numerous RIEs and had achieved WTF's proprietary second level of Lean expertise, she (or he) still couldn't say with any certainty what Lean was.

Such refreshing bits of skepticism, however, were counteracted by others in management positions who were possessed of an unseemly degree of certainty about where the company was going and what their role was in getting it there. The new manager of my department was one such booster. She was installed because upper management believed she had an eye and appetite for enforcing the Lean ideal of visual management, which was all about being able to manage by scanning the work area and all that it entailed--were the workers in their places, were tools at the ready, were daily maintenance boards visible and current, were any abnormalities on the horizon ("race to red"). The Night's Watch standing lookout for invasions of Others in *Game of Thrones* had a less daunting task. But our new manager had a zest for the job and practiced her vigilance from her desk in the far corner of the department.

After an intensive week learning about standard of work as a key component of visual management, she announced that the entire department would go on what she termed were standard company hours, 8-5, five days a week. Not to quibble, but the company had never held to any standard work hours. There was a passing reference to 8-5 in the company handbook, but that was pretty much neutralized by a directive that each department would set its hours according to its needs. In fact, the needs of the department that was the company's main income generator required work hours from 7-4. Our department was a hot bed of flex scheduling. Some of us arrived as early as 6 a.m.; some as late as 10 a.m. Some worked four-day weeks with Mondays off; some four-day weeks with Fridays off. Some schedules were due to the need to care for children; some in order to care for elderly parents; some just because some folks preferred to put in long 4-day weeks in order to have long 3-day weekends. It was all very employee-friendly...and had been for all the years I was employed there.

I realize how this may all seem disturbing to an outsider, especially an outsider peddling something called visual management, but it pretty much worked for a long time. Our department met most deadlines and produced high quality work, which drew glowing praise from upper management and outsiders. We also had our fair share of Staff of the Year award winners, among them those who had some of the most unorthodox schedules.

Historically, this change in our hours came down shortly after Yahoo CEO Marissa Mayer announced a ban on telecommuting at her company. I don't think WTF needed such encouragement to push standard work hours at WE. It was already baked into its agenda. But the Yahoo news, like the change in our hours, I believe, is indicative of how companies capitalize on difficult economic times to hammer employees into shape. It's couched in terms of doing what's best for the customer, but stripped of the rhetoric it's just old style management muscle-flexing to show the workers who's boss.

Now, what I'm about to describe happened immediately after an RIE aimed specifically at our department where what is called a Gap Analysis revealed that the department was suffering from, among other things, "unsuccessful visual management," "uneven work distribution," and "suboptimal internal organization." For each of those gaps, the high-priced team gathered in the RIE "did a root cause analysis by asking *Why* five times." They did A-3s, a calendar, drew up a completion plan—the *sensei* even pulled a few brand new tricks out of the WTF bag—"PICK" charts and the QFD tool (Quality Functional Deployment). Seal Team 6 should be so well prepared.

Yet, with all that and under the regime of standard work, within the purview of visual management (and with my own executive-approved project suggestions *for the company* idling somewhere in somebody's queue), I commenced serious work on this book. At my workstation. In plain-sight. All during the newly imposed standard work hours. With WTF placing mind-numbing emphasis on tracking every working hour, with charts galore tracking every employee with a dizzying array of arrows and stars and bars, with a pervasive and oppressive company push to get everyone on the Lean transformation bus, I sat undisturbed documenting much of what was going wrong with the process.

According to the standard of work elements detailed for each of our leaders up the chain of command, in the time I spent writing this book I should have been visited dozens of times to be asked what I was working on...how I was progressing...was I having any problems. Just one *gemba* walk should have easily raised five "why" questions. Like, why was I busily working on my personal iPad while my company iMac with its 16-inch monitor sat on my desk mostly idle for three months? Why did the vaunted Lean process allow me to not only fall through the cracks but virtually disappear from sight? Why did someone decide that Lean standards would be further advanced by leaving me with nothing to do rather than putting me to work on approved projects with long-term benefits to the company? Why did someone decide that it would be a good idea to have one of the company's most vocal critics of the Lean transformation sit without assigned work for more than 500 hours? Why, after intensive visual management and standard of work training, did our department management return to our "factory floor" so utterly blind or oblivious to the problem it was creating?

Ironically, in the three months I spent working on this book, only one person in a management position came to look over my shoulder. He looked at my iMac and said, "You can't be reading that on company time." It was Scotty, our former department director and a man inclined to trust his staff without looking over shoulders. In my 10 years of working for him, he had never once come to question my work (and, I should add, I had never once failed to deliver on any assignment he gave me). This history made an embarrassing pass between us at that moment of his calling me on my activity. I replied, "Scotty, this is the Lean material they've uploaded on our intranet and asked us to read. I can't very well read it at home."

His sheepishness gave way to bemusement. He rolled his eyes, shook his head, and walked away muttering, "This process is making fools of us all."

In the period I spent writing this book on company time, I had a total of 48 assigned hours of work and a grand total of *525* hours of unassigned work! I had become the worst of WTF's "8 Wastes"--I had become "unused human talent." As I said earlier, however, some people know how to make the most of waste...and I, fortunately, am one of them.

Occasionally I would look up from the writing of my book to peer into the adjoining meeting room where yet another WTF *sensei* would unveil yet another WTF chart that promised to sprout a beanstalk to the heavens for WE. Our managers and directors and cell leaders and such would gather around it in awe, reaching out to touch it and chattering deliriously among themselves, resembling nothing less, I'm sad to say, than the hairy humanoids in *2001: A Space Odyssey* when they found themselves in the presence of a big, black, quite baffling monolith.

RUMPLESTILTSKIN

Once there was a miller who was poor, but who had a beautiful daughter. Now it happened that he had to go and speak to the King, and in order to make himself appear important he said to him, "I have a daughter who can spin straw into gold." The King said to the miller, "That is an art which pleases me well; if your daughter is as clever as you say, bring her tomorrow to my palace, and I will see what she can do."

Of course the girl couldn't spin straw into gold and her father's empty-headed boast put her life in jeopardy. If not for the intervention of a mysterious little imp, the poor innocent girl would've been toast. As it was, she seemed hopelessly trapped between the escalating demands of a greedy king and a conniving imp. Every time the king asked for more gold, the girl would have to make more promises to the imp to do for her what she couldn't do for herself. (It may be the first instance of mission creep ever recorded, which is why we do well to pay attention to fairy tales.)

One of the first major undertakings of our company's Lean transformation came about when WTF promised to spin our building floor plan into staff flow and collaboration gold. It was a breathtaking initiative that emerged from an RIE held 6 months after WTF planted its flag on our premises. Within the strictly confined scope of an RIE, it was fairly straightforward. Under the guidance of our first *sensei*, who had not yet been promoted from Professor to Vice President Marvel, 14 representatives from throughout our 25,000 square foot, two-story building were gathered in a room for a week to discuss creating a new floor plan, according to this mission statement:

> "To redesign the administrative areas of Building 2 to accommodate logical workflows and adjacencies, create opportunities for team work and cross functional collaboration, allow for visual management and conference rooms, and make the best possible use of space."

Over the course of the week, they followed the RIE schedule as formulated by WTF—three days to examine the floor plan problem and one heavy

Thursday to brainstorm solutions to the problem, implement solutions to the problem, list actions to be taken within 30 days, define a system to sustain the changes, and prepare a presentation to the nearly 100 other people who worked in the building as to how their work spaces would be radically altered over much of a year and into the indefinite future.

Before going further, a word or two is in order about what may be the most famous office space in American history, Building 20 in Cambridge Massachusetts. In an article in *The New Yorker* magazine, Jonah Lehrer writes:

> "Building 20 became a strange, chaotic domain, full of groups who had been thrown together by chance and who knew little about one another's work. And yet, by the time it was finally demolished, in 1998, Building 20 had become a legend of innovation, widely regarded as one of the most creative spaces in the world. In the postwar decades, scientists working there pioneered a stunning list of breakthroughs, from advances in high-

speed photography to the development of the physics behind microwaves. Building 20 served as an incubator for the Bose Corporation. It gave rise to the first video game and to Chomskyan linguistics. Stewart Brand, in his study "How Buildings Learn," cites Building 20 as an example of a 'Low Road' structure, a type of space that is unusually creative because it is so unwanted and underdesigned. (Another example is the Silicon Valley garage.) As a result, scientists in Building 20 felt free to remake their rooms, customizing the structure to fit their needs. Walls were torn down without permission; equipment was stored in the courtyards and bolted to the roof. When Jerrold Zacharias was developing the first atomic clock, working in Building 20, he removed two floors in his lab to make room for a 3-story metal cylinder." [xviii]

Recreating the atmosphere of a Building 20 is the dream of the boldest of entrepreneurs. Apparently

Steve Jobs came close with his conception and execution of Apple's headquarters in Silicon Valley. A few key things about Building 20 should resonate through this chapter, and actually through this entire discussion of Lean. The first is that randomness and chaos contributed greatly to its creative energy. The second is that it started as an enormous piece of waste—the building had outgrown its intended use after World War II and was scheduled for demolition. But then a mishmash of people floating around and through M.I.T. needed office space, and a legend was made out of a space Lean would have 6S'ed out of existence before its true time had come.

Back to WE...there were problems with our grand planned redesign from the start. For one, like the mission to change our company culture, there was never an effort made to establish the existence of the problem. The problem may have been clear in the minds of a select handful of people, but that clarity was never shared with enough of staff to elicit broad buy-in. In a traditional top-down management model, this would have been standing operating procedure and therefore not an issue—what upper management wants, upper management gets. But Lean came to us advertised as a people-first methodology, with great emphasis on transparency to employees and participation by employees.

Therefore the announcement came as a shock at the Friday Report Out that the RIE had decided to remake our entire building (one of three on campus) as an open floor plan. That would have been stunning enough, but the manner in which the announcement was delivered made it worse. In another attempt to make the entire process appear like it was "up from the people," it was made by a regular employee of no particular standing--not management. It was a very brief announcement, consisting most memorably of her phrase, "I can't believe we decided to do away with all offices!"

Indeed. The new open floor plan as unveiled boasted as "a benefit" that it would reduce our current number of 23 offices to zero. It also called for an increase of conference rooms from 5 to 13, with the requisite cultural change that they would now be called *obeyas* (and a joke was born that we would now have to take off our shoes before entering a meeting). They showed photos of the RIE members standing around the giant scale model paper cutouts they had laid out on the floor to model the new floor plan. Again they eschewed the use of far more efficient tools, like interior design software, that not only would've made the RIE team's job easier but would have made the grand scheme easier to share with staff not included in the RIE. On the basis of just that one-week's work they were able to project the following "significant improvements" the new plan would yield:

- Openness
- Communication
- Confidentiality
- Visual management
- Collaboration
- Window usage

It took us in our department—which from this point on I'll call C-THRU—less than an hour to Google current research that debunked much of the work of the RIE. One of the first articles we found was by Susan Cain in the *New York Times* that questioned the basis of many of the "significant improvements" that would result from an open floor plan. She wrote:

> "The New Groupthink has overtaken our workplaces, our schools and our religious institutions. Anyone who has

ever needed noise canceling headphones in her own office or marked an online calendar with a fake meeting in order to escape yet another real one knows what I'm talking about. Virtually all American workers now spend time on teams and some 70 percent inhabit open-plan offices, in which no one has 'a room of one's own.' During the last decades, the average amount of space allotted to each employee shrank 300 square feet, from 500 square feet in the 1970s to 200 square feet in 2010.

"But it's one thing to associate with a group in which each member works autonomously on his piece of the puzzle; it's another to be corralled into endless meetings or conference calls conducted in offices that afford no respite from the noise and gaze of co-workers. Studies show that open-plan offices make workers hostile, insecure and distracted. They're also more likely to suffer from high blood pressure, stress, the flu and exhaustion. And people whose work is interrupted make 50 percent more mistakes and take twice as long to finish it." xix

Well, Lean is not about to waste space, so squeezing employees into tighter workspaces would not have made much of an impression. You would think, however, that Cain's last two points—on health and productivity—would have given our gung-ho open floor plan advocates at least some pause, but it didn't.

Another article was the result of a study by Knoll Industries, which because of its stake in office design and furnishings wanted to find the most objective and useful data on the subject of open floor plans. Knoll's report read in part:

> "Generally speaking, moving a worker from a private office to an open plan workstation is perceived as a takeaway, which in large part explains the difficulty organizations encounter when trying to migrate from enclosed workspace to open workspace standards. Additionally, while many corporations have spent more than a

decade attempting to eliminate status associations with the physical work environment, more than half of the workers that participated in our study acknowledge that the kind and quality of space one is given is related to one's status within the organization.

"Simply placing workers in an open environment, without attending to work process, does not mean they will collaborate, or that productivity increases will be realized." [xx]

Not as dramatic an objection as health and productivity, but there was a clear warning there that work process must be integrated into any change to a work environment or projected significant improvements will be neutralized. Whatever our new work process would be in the new environment had not taken shape yet, though that process was definitely in the drawing board stage. Still, to push forward with the floor plan before the process seemed more than a little like putting the cart before the horse. As employees adapted to the new process they may have been better able to appreciate the need for a new floor plan, but no one driving this effort seemed to realize or care that this might be the case.

Defense Exhibit C in our effort to push back against the coming reconfiguration was the result of an extensive study of 65,000 workers worldwide on the subject of open floor plans conducted by the University of California, Berkeley. As reported by John Tierney in *The New York Times*:

> "...More than half of office workers are dissatisfied with the level of 'speech privacy,' making it the leading complaint in offices everywhere.
>
> "'In general, people do not like the acoustics in open offices,' said John Goins, the leader of the survey conducted by Berkeley's Center for the Built Environment. 'The noisemakers aren't so bothered by the lack of privacy, but most people are not happy, and designers are finally starting to pay attention to the problem.'
>
> "The original rationale for the open-plan office, aside from saving space and money, was to foster communication

among workers, the better to coax them to collaborate and innovate. But it turned out too much communication sometimes had the opposite effect: a loss of privacy...." [xxi]

It is significant that the RIE chose to highlight "confidentiality" as a significant improvement that would result from the open floor plan when there was this massive study readily available from a world-class research institution challenging the merits of that supposition on the facts. How could data that significant not enter into the discussion? How could a *sensei* or teacher or whatever the hell you want to call yourself not make sure such information was part of the conversation? It would, it seemed to me, be like ignoring the fact that 65,000 Toyota cars were having serious problems with floor mats and proceeding to install them anyway.

It was bad enough that the most major company physical change since our 100-mile relocation a decade earlier was undertaken without consideration of these arguments. But when we in C-THRU presented these articles and this reputable third party evidence, we were told that there was countervailing evidence "out there" that made the case *for* the open floor plan. But no one felt compelled to present that evidence to our department or as far as we could tell to anyone else. This significant reconfiguration would proceed with little to zero outside input under the guidance of a second *sensei* (who I will dub The Boy Wonder for his ability to rearrange buildings with just a wave of his hand).

To her credit, the VP of our division, who I will christen here (without sarcasm) as Vice President Scattergood, gamely faced our department when we made our last stand against the proposed makeover. She heard out our case with magnanimity and humor. At one point she joked that the company's relationship with WTF was like a Vegas wedding. To which I responded, "Yes, and we're the children who've stumbled into your room wondering who the new man is in your bed and why's he telling us how to organize our room?"

The meeting did not end on a happy note, however. When we had finally pushed her far enough, she took management's default position of deferring to WTF. "I've discussed your concerns with The Boy Wonder," she said (using his real name). "And I begged him to tell me this will work. And he said, 'Trust me.'"

> *Miyagi*: We make sacred pact. I promise
> teach karate to you. You promise learn. I
> say. You do. No questions.

As the subsequent months unfolded, our entire building was subjected to unprecedented disruption. The company had to bring in numerous outside contractors to demolish old walls and erect new walls, rewire, re-plumb, refurbish, readjust, realign, reallocate, rearrange, restore, reassemble, redecorate, and just generally redo. The end result was a mess. What had been a fairly standard and orderly work environment ended up looking like a cross between a telemarketing boiler room and a warehouse. It was every bit as unfriendly to productivity as our research said it would be, and it was ugly. The disaster was evident enough even for some of its in-house advocates to recognize, though The Boy Wonder remained unshakable in his belief that *his* vision was absolutely right for workers doing jobs he had never done in a company he had known for mere months. It was such an obvious disaster, in fact, that a make-good RIE was scheduled to deal with its failings.

Oddly, when the RIE was convened to deal with the nearly open rebellion against the reconfiguration, the atmosphere in the room was as passive and pliant as it was in the original RIE that created the debacle. Our company president picked up on this as soon as she set foot in the RIE. She demanded to know why the RIE did not include any of the more vocal critics of the new floor plan. She called Vice President Scattergood who was abroad on business travel and Scotty, our C-THRU boss at the time, and insisted that more of our department attend the RIE since we were in the vanguard of the dissent. And since I personally was in the vanguard of the vanguard, my name was put forward as the most representative voice. The *sensei* leading the RIE—yet a fourth sensei assigned to our division since the transformation had begun a year earlier rejected my addition to the group on the grounds that I was too passionate on the issue to be helpful.

News that the most knowledgeable and vocal opponent of the open floor plan had been excluded from this review spread quickly, unhindered by offices or walls, and solidified the slow, but steadily shaping impression that the entire Lean process was fixed.

Fixed or not, the make-good RIE revealed no less than 40 issues created by the building makeover that required attention. According to the new mission statement:

> "The redesign of Building 2 has created an all new workplace that will enable better communication, team work, and collaboration. However with numerous staff members relocated to the new open office environment, the old methods for interacting no longer suffice. Additional refinements are needed to make the workspace as functional as possible."

And here's the real beauty of "continuous improvement"—you get to say this is all part of the process. Among the things which would require improvement, continuous or otherwise, as delineated during the RIE, were:

- Workstation document privacy
- Noise
- Glare
- Conference room...oops, *obeya*...scheduling
- Traffic through open executive areas
- Traffic around and through work areas

- Multiple, distracting conversations
- A men's room door that directly opened on to the workstation of two female employees

Add to the list a break room that divided two departments and the entire open floor plan in two, thus keeping departments that were separated still separated and unleashing lunchtime noise and odors on two work areas at once.

The list of issues was divided into "Just Do Its" and projects. Six months later, 18 of the 40 items remained undone, despite the RIE mandate to complete them in 30 days. And every lunch hour was another reminder of how miserably the effort had been conceived and executed as the smells of sushi, day-old spaghetti, and hard-boiled eggs combined and wafted over the expanse of open space like emissions from the local gas works.

At the end of the Friday Report Out, the usual opportunity for questions from staff not involved in the RIE was omitted—yet another oversight in this allegedly highly calibrated process. As a result, I had to submit my question to our company Lean team and upper management via email. My question pivoted off a quotation from leading European Lean authority

Michael Ballé, who had addressed a recent Lean summit in the UK, where he had stated, "The basic rule of thumb is that lean should increase common trust—if it decreases common trust it's just plain wrong (no ifs, ands, or buts)."

So I asked our people at WE a three-part question:

- Did they agree with Ballé's assessment on the importance of building common trust?
- If so, had they established metrics to determine if common trust at WE was increasing or decreasing?
- If they had not, could they establish such a metric as we moved into the second year of our Lean transformation?

THE SEVEN DWARFS

Just whistle while you work
And cheerfully together we can tidy up the place
So hum a merry tune
It won't take long
When there's a song
To help you set the pace

Even if you can't name each of Snow White's seven dwarfs, you know enough to know that each of their names indicates a unique trait that separates them from one another. Most savvy employers know that their workforce—like the dwarfs working that fairy tale gold mine—come in a diversity of character and personality. Each workforce consists of its own versions of Doc, Grumpy, Happy, Sleepy, Bashful, Sneezy, and Dopey. Most employers would like to have more Docs and Happys and fewer Grumpys and Dopeys, but that diversity is unavoidable, barring some science fiction intervention that turns all your workers into contented, productive automatons. And the key to effective management is making that diversity work for you.

WTF was not so blind as to miss this reality. WTF was cognizant of the lack of homogeneity in the modern workforce and in fact recognized three distinct groups:

Artisan—individuals who process with their own resources and personal standards; collaboration for them is almost impossible; their output is highly variable

Craft—workers who process according to broadly agreed standards that allow collaboration on bigger projects; they require a full set of equipment; their output is also variable

Mass—workers who process according to division of labor, economies of scale, centers of excellence; they require standard work and "push" to clearly define and streamline their flow lines

Not as colorful as Happy and Sleepy of course, but that's not an unreasonable breakdown. There seems to be a built-in problem as far as Lean goes, however, or at least the WTF version of Lean. According to WTF, artisan and craft workers are not as easily integrated into the Lean process as Mass workers are. In fact WTF sees artisan and craft workers mostly as obstacles to Lean. To quote from one of its in-house publications that WTF made available to us at WE and encouraged us to read:

> "...In a Mass-type process it will seem a small, but generally positive journey to move to JIT [Just in time] processes, but for a person in an Artisan or Craft-based process it will not. Why? Most people who work in Craft-based processes unconsciously see personal value and skill in being able to negotiate the waste that is a fundamental part of their work. In many cases they are rated and rewarded for this ability. Not only have they grown accustomed to waste being there, but it often defines them as a worker. People who work in Craft-type process environments rarely work in a true team in the JIT-flow sense of the word...."

This created a real problem for my particular department at WE. Although none of us were Artisans in the sense of suffering for our art in Bohemian garrets, we were far closer to the Craft designation than the Mass, which meant that we were, *prima facie*, not ideally suited for Lean transformation. This probably accounts for the fact that our department, C-THRU, was most resistant to the building reconfiguration described in the last chapter and most critical of the Lean transformation overall. WTF deserves credit, I guess, for correctly singling out our "type" as the ones who would present the greatest challenge in pushing through the cultural changes they sought. As to whether they deserve credit for how they chose to meet that challenge or prepared our management to understand that challenge is the overriding question of this chapter.

The problem began to manifest itself in the very first RIE that included members of our department. One of my co-workers, who for the purposes of this book I will baptize Toto II after Dorothy's dog in *The Wizard of Oz*, raised the question: *Why?* As in, why had the company decided to go in the direction of a wholesale Lean transformation? I was informed by reliable sources that Toto II framed the question in a most confrontational manner. Having not been present, but knowing Toto II as I do, I could easily accept this characterization. But if I may go back to the original Toto, he wasn't terribly polite in exposing the fraud of the Wizard of Oz either. Sometimes congeniality and skepticism do not go hand in hand. In any case, the question itself struck me as altogether fundamental and fitting. After all, the process we were about to embark upon, we were told, encouraged the Socratic method of asking questions. In fact, WTF made a rather big deal of the fact that it thought so much of the Socratic method that it built in as an essential part of its process what it called "The 5 Whys." WTF claimed that the act of asking "why" 5 times is an effective problem solving technique. Why 5 times and not 3 times or 10 times or 32 times would be a question I'd like to ask, but that's beside the point. From what I did understand, the point was to get people to dig deeper in problem solving and not just settle for the first answer that comes to mind. That seems a worthy habit for people to develop, regardless of the eventual number of "whys" that are asked.

The far greater point, it seemed to me, was who gets to ask why, however many. It was clear that from

WTF's view the power to ask why belonged to the *sensei*. As company leaders and managers mastered the force of Lean, they too would get to ask why. The reaction to Toto II's question, however, left little doubt that the right to ask why did not extend to staff. Professor Marvel ejected Toto II from the Emerald City that was the RIE. I've heard the defense of this action—Toto II's attitude was creating negativity in the room; the question as to why we were doing a Lean transformation had been answered months earlier by upper management; the bus was now moving forward and this was neither the time nor place for asking why.

The episode reminded me of my days as a high school English teacher. In 10 years, not a year went by in which I wasn't greeted by at least one sour student who made a very big verbal or non-verbal show of not wanting to be there—*why do we have to learn this, what good will it do me, why do I have to be in school anyway.* You learn early on if you want to keep teaching that when you're confronted with that student, you take a deep breath and you answer the questions. You tell the student that the why he has to be there was determined by a society that decided for its own well being that it wanted as many of its citizens as educated as possible. You tell the student that even though this is not a job training course or a family-counseling course, you hope to teach thinking and learning skills that will be useful in the student's professional and personal life. You tell the student that they must be there by either law or their parents' will and that the requirement is beyond the power of either the teacher or student to alter, so let's try to make the most of it in the time we must spend together. And as you tell your dissatisfied student these things, as much as you hope to reach him or her, you know you're answering in a full and earnest fashion for the other students in the class. You're answering for the ones who may have the same questions on their minds but are too polite or timid to ask. You're taking the time to answer because the challenge usually comes up the first day or week of class, and you have to set the tone for the rest of the semester. You're demonstrating that you're not afraid to answer tough questions, and you're letting your students know that they shouldn't be afraid to ask tough questions. Invariably I found that in doing this the other students would subsequently become your biggest allies in dealing with more difficult students.

None of that happens of course if you eject the student from the classroom. Quite the opposite. You reveal yourself as either a coward or a tyrant. This is a simple truth that one would think that anyone deserving of the title *sensei* would have mastered early on. And though the incident had a negative impact on staff outside of the RIE, the damage may have been limited if the attitude the incident exposed did not get continually reinforced throughout our Lean transformation.

As I researched further into Lean for the purposes of this book, I realized that it has pretty much a schizophrenic attitude toward workers in general. On the one hand, there are statements of belief and pronouncements of practices that would lift the spirit of the long-dead, legendary union figure Joe Hill. In *What I Learned from Ohno*, a talk delivered in January 1998, Michikazu Tanaka, a former executive of Daihatsu Motors and a chief disciple of the acknowledged godfather of Lean, Taiichi Ohno, said:

"In my talk, I have covered only some of the most trying incidents and most gratifying incidents in our work with Ohno-san. I hope that my remarks have conveyed the most important message: that motivation is everything. Tools and methods are secondary. Any tool or method will work if people are motivated. And no tool or method will work if people are not motivated. That's what I learned from Ohno-san." [xxii]

In 2001 Toyota published *The Toyota Way*, which made explicit that "respect for people" was one of its guiding principles:

"The 'Respect for People' principle is deceptive in that it seems very easy to understand and apply, but it is not. Most mid- and senior-level managers think they know what 'Respect for People' means, but it is clear from leadership behaviors, common business performance metrics, company policies, management's decisions, and sometimes even corporate strategy, that they do not." [xxiii]

At The Lean Enterprise Institute's "Gemba Coach" blog, Michael Ballé consistently and passionately advocates for the value of workers in Lean transformations. Here is an excerpt from one of his columns:

> "Dear Gemba Coach,
>
> I appreciate your frequent discussions about the value of respect in order to be lean. Unfortunately my company has embarked on a lean program that is anything but respectful. Competent people are stigmatized as 'concrete heads' whenever they disagree with anything the lean coaches come up with, even when their prescriptions make absolutely no business sense. What used to be a good atmosphere for work is now poisoned by resentment and distrust. How can that be compatible with the 'respect' message of lean?
>
> Gemba Coach:
>
> Ouch. I wish I could say you're in a unique situation, but unfortunately, I have heard of many firms where this

does happen, and have even seen a few during gemba visits. So you're probably observing something very real, and I'm sorry that you have to go through it. Let me start by clarifying 'respect' as I understand it...In lean, respect means 'respect for the development of the person to his or her fullest ability'...This doesn't necessarily involve being polite...Respect is mostly about the boss' good intentions towards you, even if somehow this intention is shown awkwardly...." xxiv

Even WTF has enlightened words to say on the subject. One of the slides from Vice President Marvel's orientation PowerPoint claimed that WTF's objective was to promote:

"Non Judgmental-Non Blaming Behavior--To create a highly effective and performing culture it is key to develop trust. In doing so it is imperative to be honest and open in communications but refrain from judgmental and blaming statements and behavior."

So there is a long, admirable thread running through Lean for developing respect for people, or more specifically workers. Yet throughout that history, there have also been expressions of impatience with workers as the sometimes-unpleasant variable in the process. In *What I Learned from Ohno*, Michikazu Tanaka describes Ohno's prescription for passing Lean ideals on:

> "The way to pass this spirit on to the next generation is to go out into the workplace and scold people. If someone screws up, take them into the workplace, show them exactly what's gone wrong, and give them a good scolding. When someone gets a scolding in the workplace while looking at what's actually happened, they can't make any excuses. The scolding presents ... a higher standard to meet." [xxv]

Like *gemba* and *kaizen* and *sensei*, I don't really think scolding workers translates very well to Western cultures, especially US workers. Although I never heard the word scold come from WTF, in most of two years there certainly were multiple actions that translated into a scolding. The mere fact that "at-will" to describe our employment status was tossed around more often in Lean's first year than in all my previous years with WE speaks to that.

At another point in *What I Learned from Ohno*, Tanaka says:

> "Another thing Ohno-san said about kaizen was that we should never listen to the shop veterans. 'They just get in the way of kaizen,' he'd say. '...Wisdom is born from the ideas of novices. The veterans will spout off about what's possible and what's not possible on the basis of their experience and a tiny bit of knowledge. And when the veterans speak, everyone else keeps quiet. So kaizen can't even get started.'" xxvi

If Ohno-san had been named coach of an American sports franchise and came in with that attitude, he would have become known as Ohno-stupid in about a month—and out of a job in a year. You can't get away with that attitude in areas where workers have rare and special skills...like sports, software development or medicine. You can only get away with it where you view workers as expendable. Ohno-san made this statement some 60 years ago in a factory where such odious attitudes were prevalent. But it has been passed down through Lean as part of his legacy. With reverence for the man in Lean circles bordering on the religious, one can imagine what a so-called *sensei* with little sense would do upon latching on to it—or some Lean transforming company middle manager prone to get drunk on the mere whiff of power over other people's lives.

It is a blatantly ageist sentiment, and there is clear evidence that some Lean practitioners are contemptuous of veteran employees. Aside from the legal ramifications of that sentiment in the US, it seems outrageous and counterproductive for a philosophy looking to forge an ideal work environment based largely on the input of workers. Cavalierly dismissing the input of your most experienced hands points down a path for travelling on reinvented wheels rather than continuous improvement.

For all its professed cultivation of respect for the factory floor (or at least the freshest, most malleable voices from the factory floor), Lean often seems tone deaf—sometimes spectacularly so—to the input of workers. In 2010, for instance, the fiasco that was the opening of the much-ballyhooed, multi-billion pound, Lean-driven new Heathrow Terminal 5 was traced directly to Lean "process engineers" who chose to ignore the input of veteran employees. As a result, on what was to be a grand opening day, flights were cancelled, delayed, or diverted to other terminals; hundreds of bags were lost. It was embarrassing and bad enough to lead to a government inquiry, where Union Shop Steward Iggy Vaid gave this testimony before the British House of Commons:

> "We raised [worker concerns] with our senior management team especially in British Airways. ... [Their response was to] involve what we call process engineers who came in and decided what type of process needed to be installed. They only wanted the union to implement that process and it was decided by somebody else, not the

people who really worked it. The fact is that they paid lip service to, ignored or did not implement any suggestion we made." xxvii

I like my British comrade's use of "process engineers." Throughout this book I've been struggling to come up with a term less offensive to them than vendors and less offensive to me than *sensei*. Because of my decade-long teaching experience, I have some idea of what it takes to be a teacher, and I was just not seeing it in the parade of individuals WTF had been sending our way to counsel and guide us through such a profound transformation. What I saw was a group of men so enamored of the processes they promote that whether anybody cares, needs, trusts, applies, or appreciates those processes is beyond their comprehension. Engineers love how things work, and that's a good thing—good for them and good for the people who hire them and depend upon them to make things work. But engineers, generally, are not attuned to what makes non-engineers work and love their work.

The Lean obsession with "waste" is one glaring example. And again I give WTF credit for calling it accurately in saying about artisans and craft workers: "Not only have they grown accustomed to waste being there, but it often defines them as a worker." I'm not going to go sniffing for the truffle of insult where none exists, so I won't interpret that to mean that WTF believes that a certain type of worker, like a pig, prefers to muck around in his or her own waste. I take it to mean that WTF considers certain types of workers as being functional enough around inefficiencies that they can tolerate them beyond the abilities of more Mass type workers, if you will, to tolerate them. This in turn allows—let's call them— privileged wastes to persist and grow to the ultimate detriment of those workers who cannot perform optimally under less than optimal conditions. This can manifest itself in the most obvious way with, say, an IT person who can bury his desk under cables, drives, modems, catalogs, and coffee cups and still manage to perform his job at a high level. This does not compute with the process engineer who believes that not only does the "waste" surrounding the IT person interfere with that person's job performance, but with the job performance of others in the company. Yet anyone who works in a company with such a person knows that time after time he or she is able to come through to solve someone else's crisis, and often it is with the aid of a so-called piece of waste off the heap. The process engineer wants to see all the items in the workstation neatly organized, within reach, up-to-date, and designated for a particular purpose. Furthermore, he believes that in an environment of ideal flow and collaboration the editor or the graphic artist should, in the IT person's absence, be able to step into the workstation and access the proper tool for solving a problem. Dopey can, in practice, become Doc.

This goes beyond mere standards of neatness, it goes to the heart of how certain people...certain workers...derive satisfaction from their jobs. People actually get satisfaction out of finding workarounds to problems, enjoy making use of others' garbage, take pride in doing a job that is not so easily transferable to anyone else. This gets at one of the fundamental contradictions in Lean that I believe will continue to nag at it as it tries to transition from purely manufacturing environments to more sophisticated work environments. I believe that the Lean process engineers genuinely want workers to be happy and productive—even WTF's process engineers probably want it in spite of their evident obtuseness. But I also believe that they see the path to that happiness and productivity running through them and their processes. There is an inherent arrogance to that thinking that undermines all the flattering things they may have to say about respecting workers. The true teacher knows that such respect grows out of understanding the diverse levels of skill, motivation, and compatibility among students/workers. If you tie your efforts to the goal of creating a smooth, self-improving, optimally interchangeable process, you have hitched your wagon to a delusion, which will ultimately doom your efforts to failure and the workers you believe you're helping to debilitating frustration.

In an assessment of the failure of Aardvark, a company that followed the Lean blueprint to the letter and was supposed to be a model of a Lean start-up, Glen Thrope at a Harvard Business School blog wrote:

> "And yet, Aardvark's final product was underwhelming. The dynamic between the service's question askers and answerers didn't quite work...Though

the product was ultimately acquired for a hefty sum, Aardvark fell far short of the original ambitions of its founders.

"In the end, the Aardvark case does point out a hole in lean...[it] is not an all-inclusive instruction... Though it can be a useful tool for executing on a high level vision, Lean offers little in the way of guidance when it comes to developing that vision.

"Where, then, does this vision come from? I think the answer lies in an unscientific jumble of intuition, creativity, experience, and a bit of zaniness – in short, the imagination. Lean in many ways underplays the importance of imagination, and yet the case of Aardvark reminds us that it is absolutely critical." xxviii

MIDAS TOUCH

And while Midas was rejoicing in great wealth, his servants set a table for his meal, with many dainties and with needful bread: but when he touched the bread with his right hand, it instantly stiffened to gold; when he tried to bite a tender bit of meat, it flashed with yellow shreds and flakes of gold as soon as his teeth touched it. And as he thirst for wine, it, too, turned in his astonished mouth to liquid gold. Confounded by this strange misfortune—rich yet wretched—he became anxious to escape from his unhappy circumstance. He had come to hate all he had so lately longed for.

Be careful of what you wish for may be one of the most under-appreciated axioms of our time. In Beverly Silver's paper on the history of the auto industry's relationship with its workers, she writes:

> "As an October 8, 1992, New York Times article noted: 'Because the [US] automobile industry has largely adopted the Japanese system of keeping

production inventories low, strikes at part plants have a much broader impact than in the past . . . The ability of the union to cripple production by putting only a few thousand workers on strike is a way of imposing costs on the company that may outweigh the savings from job cuts...' There are already numerous cases where transport strikes and supplier strikes have led to widespread assembly plant closings in the southern Great Lakes states under the just-in-time system....

"Strikes at suppliers can lead to equally rapid disruption of production. For example: 'When workers at Delco Electronics plant in Kokomo, Indiana, went on strike in November 1986, GM assembly plants around the country were closed. Because radios from the plant were being shipped on a just-in-time basis, assembly plants had little inventory on hand with which to work once the strike began. The strike was called to protest Delco's sourcing of some work to a plant in Mexico. GM felt compelled to return the work to Kokomo in order to get a supply of radios flowing into the assembly line plants again.'

"In sum, the just-in-time system continues to put as much--or more--disruptive power in the hands of workers as the more traditional Fordist organization of production. On the other hand, in Japan, where these methods were pioneered and have been developed to their fullest, workers have not routinely exercised these powers. The key seems to be the guarantee of lifetime employment to the upper rungs of the workforce (those with the most disruptive power) and a concentration of the pressures of low wages and insecure employment on the lower rungs of the workforce (those without significant disruptive power). However, can this process be maintained in the coming decades?" [xxix]

As with imagination, Lean, at least as practiced by WTF, underestimates the power of workers in the success of any company. I kept hoping that WE would not make that mistake. The day after I sent my memo to upper management asking if our Lean experience was building trust, cared about building trust, and had any plans for building trust, I received a call from Vice President Scattergood asking if we could meet for a half-hour over coffee. I took it as a promising sign that our "factory floor" would not be ignored. However, when we met she very quickly launched into what I read as a filibuster of our 30 minutes, comprised mostly of a message delivered in a number of different ways, but all coming down to the same thing: this Lean transformation WE had undertaken was serious, long-term, and unalterable. At about the 20 minute mark I had determined that at the first pause I would thank her for her time and officially end my kibitzing on the direction the company was heading. Then the pause came, and I couldn't let the opportunity pass. I didn't know when, if ever, I'd get a one-on-one with her again, so I jumped in.

I said I wanted to make one thing clear before our meeting ended. That one thing was that excluding me from the building makeover RIE was immaterial to me personally, but I believed strongly that management should know how that and numerous other little things that had happened since WTF arrived were having a widespread adverse impact on company morale. I went into some detail about those other little things and ended by saying that it was my view, from the factory floor, that this developing morale issue could be the ultimate undoing of our Lean transformation.

In *Thinking Fast and Slow*, Daniel Kahneman writes:

> "There is a direct link from more precise gossip at the water cooler to better decisions. Decision makers are sometimes better able to imagine the voice of present gossipers and future critics than to hear the hesitant voices of their own doubts. They will make better choices when they trust their critics to be sophisticated and fair, and when they expect their decision to be judged by how it was made, not only by how it turned out." [xxx]

I was doing my best to be sophisticated and fair in bringing her the latest gossip on the Lean transformation from the company water coolers. She had a reputation for being both a good listener and what we call a people person. And even though that had been my personal experience with her, I was still shocked at how much she changed from the time she had started talking to the time I stopped talking. She had gone from hard-nosed executive who had basically come to read me the riot act to humble co-worker questing for help with a very knotty problem. She neither got defensive nor confrontational over my report of spreading low morale, but instead went straight to asking for my suggestions for solving the problem.

To that, I reiterated a suggestion I had made in one of our recent company open meetings that WE survey its workers on how well they thought the Lean transformation was going. I argued that since most of us were both customers of WTF as well as workers on WE's "factory floor," it might be useful to take a reading on what so much expenditure of time and money was yielding. At the time I made that suggestion, The Boy Wonder was present and expressed his strong opposition to such a survey, proclaiming that it would only open the door to what he described as more complaining. One man's complaints of course are another's Socratic questions. To my pleasant surprise, Vice President Scattergood ended our meeting with the promise to give my survey idea more thought.

The next day she surprised me even more by calling and inviting me to join her on a tour of three area companies that had been engaged in Lean much longer than WE had. I was amused and intrigued by the invitation. I had been building a reputation as anti-Lean, though I was constantly trying to clarify that it was not Lean *per se* that I was against but Lean as WTF was delivering it to our company. This tour would give me the chance to test how open my own mind really was on the subject.

The first company on the tour was different from ours in that it was primarily a manufacturing environment, Lean's natural habitat. So it was no big surprise to see how much better a fit it was. The factory floor was impeccably clean and organized, and the workers seemed to be comfortable in their environment. So comfortable, in fact, that at one stop on the tour when I commented upon how neat the particular area was, the manager of it said that we should've seen the mess it was the week before they 6S'd it in preparation for the tour. "You mean you don't 6S daily?" I asked. They laughed. I appreciated the fact that they had a sense of humor about the process, something that was increasingly in short supply back at WE under WTF.

At one point, VP Scattergood asked how much orientation they had gone through in preparation for their Lean transformation. The answer was that every employee had gone through a week getting immersed in Lean language and philosophy. It was a stunning contrast to the hour-and-half PowerPoint presentation WTF had provided WE employees.

As the tour passed through the administrative area of this company, I was struck not only by the absence of charts like the ones that had papered over every available wall space at our company, but by the presence of cubes and offices. In the Q &A that followed, I asked the lead Lean person from that company if the issue of open floor plan had come up during their Lean transformation. He said it had come up briefly in the beginning, but the employees immediately raised strong objection, and that was the end of it. And that should have been the end of the answer, but Vice President Marvel was also on the tour, and he raised his hand to ask our guide to speak to the benefits of an open floor plan. Our guide registered the question for the non sequitur that it was, but politely answered that he supposed open floor plans promoted collaboration.

The next company we visited was a biotech company with a large industrial component. Again, the impression on the factory floor was the same...clean, organized, and apparent compatibility with the work force. The use of charts seemed judicious and comprehensible, even to outsiders. The person in charge of the company's Lean effort said that almost all Lean related charts and other materials are available on the company intranet so people can access them immediately from their computers and not have to walk—gemba, or otherwise—all over this very large complex to review and consult.

And once again, I was struck by the presence of cubes and offices—festooned with personal items—at another company that had been at Lean many years longer than WE had. And again, because this was a hot button issue with me, I asked our guide if they had ever thought about going to an open floor plan. She said they did in the beginning but upper management had left the final decision to their in-house Lean team, which decided against it. She then joked that company VPs still thank them for not calling their bluff and leaving them with their offices. The difference between the Lean transformation at these companies and at WE was getting more striking with each stop—both in style and substance.

The third company presented a similar picture to the first two. By this stop, however, I was ready to move on to my second hot button issue—the survey. It was here that we were shown the company's proprietary problem solving matrix that revealed that the credit department was not the cause of the bottleneck in accounts receivables (discussed earlier). After his presentation, I asked the Lean leader of that company if that matrix was any good for solving soft problems like company morale. He replied that they survey their people all the time for how things are going. And, he added, they don't stop if 75% of the workforce is satisfied, but 25% is not. They want to know why that 25% is dissatisfied and whether it's caused by something that could spread or be corrected, so they dig down. He said it's surprising how you can actually mine data that addresses morale issues. Sometimes you find that a new person has been added to a group and it's not a good fit, or someone in a group is going through a hard time outside of work and it's affecting the workplace, or a process change has been made that is proving frustrating. It was a remarkably enlightened and enlightening answer that I made a point of detailing it on my iPad, which was becoming increasingly indispensable as the journal of my personal Lean journey.

The tour actually ended with representatives from those three companies and other companies either considering Lean or already doing Lean coming to WE. The moment that stands out most for me was when Vice President Marvel addressed the entire group to give an update on our Lean transformation. When he got to the subject of our building reconfiguration, it was clear the tour had injected a bit of defensiveness into the usual certainty of his manner. He told the group and the WE managers who had now joined us that WTF doesn't usually advocate such large-scale changes as the building reconfiguration until 3 to 5 years into the transformation process. To which one of WE's directors who had been on the front lines of the blowback against the building remodel, blurted out, "Now you tell us!"

VP Marvel, much resembling the Wizard when Toto pulled back the curtain, sheepishly replied, "Well, I left WTF and went to work for WE full time before the change was actually implemented, so it was another *sensei* who pushed it through, not me." It's hard to choose a single moment that would be most symbolic of all that was going wrong with our Lean transformation, but that one—with Marvel throwing The Boy Wonder under the Lean bus—would definitely be among my top five.

A few days later Vice President Scattergood asked to meet to get my feedback on the tour. I pulled out my iPad and told her that my notes mostly focused on the issues that had been most salient to me through the year. The first was the difference in time allotted to orienting employees. The second was the use of digital capabilities to replace the excessive reliance on the paper and white board charts. The third, of course, was the open floor plan. And the fourth was that all of these companies had entrusted their Lean transformations to their own people. They had sent them off for 10 weeks of training and then allowed them to apply that training to their experiences and know-how about the company. If the company culture was going to be remade, it was going to be remade by people who fully understood the culture in the first place and were themselves not aliens to it.

Vice President Scattergood was unfailingly attuned to my ideas and practical suggestions. And taking a cue from "The Gemba Coach," I, at all times, tried to frame whatever my input was in terms of Lean practices and tradition. In *What I Learned from Ohno* Michikazu Tanaka quotes one of Ohno's prime disciples at Toyota as telling him:

> "Good kaizen depends on the active cooperation of your employees. You might think you're on the right track. But unless your employees are taking part actively, you'll never get the full potential of the improvements. That's why we're going to keep working on this

until the people in the workplace think we've got it right." [xxxi]

At ThedaCare, the Wisconsin non-profit hospital where Lean has had one of its most notable non-manufacturing successes, Roger Gerard, the hospital's Chief Learning Officer and one the principal guides of its Lean transformation says:

> "We measure employee engagement annually, through a survey process designed and conducted by the Advisory Board, out of Washington DC. This survey includes 60+ indicators, two of which we track very closely, due to their power to predict engagement based on our statistical analysis. These two indicators focus on whether people really know what is expected of them, and whether they feel they make a difference in their work." [xxxii]

I continued to push for a survey of our staff on the impact of the Lean transformation despite the objections of WTF's process engineers. And finally Vice President Scattergood gave me the go-ahead to devise a survey. Frankly I would have preferred to have an outside party devise and administer such a survey, but I was happy to be making such a major inroad. So I went to work on devising some questions that I thought would elicit useful staff feedback. VP Scattergood and I went back and forth on various drafts of the questions in what was a wholly productive and collaborative process. We discussed specifics as to how and when the survey would be conducted and how it would be framed so staff understood it as a reset of the Lean initiative rather than full-scale abandonment of it. This would be a clear signal that the company was breaking from the distinct impression of our first year that staff's only option was to get on the Lean bus or get out. This would be the beginning of a new Lean era at WE, emphasizing engagement of staff.

The new direction took another highly promising turn when our top Lean people emerged from their first RIE of 2013 and presented their Report Out to staff. First off, they presented a slide that openly admitted to doing a poor job of getting staff buy-in. Then, as they do for all the Report Outs, they offered two sketches—one portraying where they were now and one portraying where they planned to be in the future. These sketches tend to be an effort to put a happy face on whatever pain the participants in the RIE went through during the week. There's a lot of the old "accentuate the positive" about them that sometimes forces awkward moments as people struggle to give public testimony to what WTF called "insights," which often came down to proclamations of how much they enjoyed working with fellow employees they had never known before. Like midnight on New Year's Eve, everyone seemed to be under a lot of pressure to be enthusiastic. What was astonishing to me about this particular Current State Sketch was how honest it was. In it, our top people acted out being on a bus that was rambling aimlessly. Each had a different idea of where they wanted to go and how the bus should be driven. VP Scattergood, good sport that she is, was the hapless driver of the bus, who, when it finally came to a stop, had to sadly announce to the others that they had never left the parking lot.

I viewed the sketch as a healthy admission that things in the first year had not gone well, delivered with admirable humor and humility. I thought it bode well for implementing the plans VP Scattergood and I had discussed for the coming reset. I did not realize that the one minor flaw I found in the sketch segment of the Report Out would turn out to be a major impediment to any chance at a reset. In the Future State portion of the sketch, The Boy Wonder assumed the role of GPS, confidently directing the bus toward its destination. I joked that he should have been playing the GPS in the Current State sketch instead where the bus went nowhere. Closer to reality, he would've been yelling at the frazzled bus driver, "Go Faster! Faster! Drive with your eyes closed. Take your hands off the wheel. Let me drive!"

The joke was on me, as subsequent months revealed the real message of the sketch was that WE had not listened well enough to the process engineers, and if things were going to get corrected moving forward, WE would have to do a better job of paying attention to WTF.

My idea of surveying the entire staff on how well the Lean transformation was going died. Instead they introduced surveys to RIE participants, limiting the questions to how well things went in each RIE. With participants small in number and easily identifiable, anonymity was compromised. Plus, the surveys were conducted under the tight supervision of VP Marvel, the person with the most vested interest in the outcome of the surveys.

The open floor plan continued to be a dismal reminder of how badly things had gone in the first year. It was supposed to eliminate silos but only served to create new ones. It was supposed to promote collaboration between departments, but had negligible impact there. For instance, I had come up with a number of ideas for our new website launch, which was being jointly run by my department leader and marketing. I submitted my ideas to both. My department leader ignored them; marketing responded enthusiastically. So I met with marketing separately to discuss how to bridge the gap. Mind you, this meant walking to an entirely different building, so the open floor plan did not, as promised, create spatial flow between departments...nor could it have without totally leveling the entire three-building complex and rebuilding it from the ground up.

Regardless, my ideas got lost in a turf war between C-Thru and marketing—a turf war that had existed long before Lean and persisted through Lean (RIE-inspired insights about the value of working well with others notwithstanding). I suspect the same war would exist long after Lean and right up until the day arrived when people issues rather than process issues were finally and fully addressed.

What the open floor plan did succeed in doing was significantly increase staff stress level since closed-door meetings—always a cause for a jump in office stress levels—became rampant. To alleviate the distraction factor, workers were continually summoned into designated meeting rooms to discuss everything from the most confidential to the most incidental subjects, so every closed door meeting became cause for anxiety—warranted or not. Then employees had to constantly run out of the area to take or make calls—another jolt to the anxiety level for caller and co-worker alike. But the open floor plan was not completely devoid of comedy—in eliminating wall space, the process engineers no longer had a convenient place to hang each of their new charts. Thus windows with once stunning ocean views got papered over with crude handmade charts and Post-it notes.

From the beginning, our entire Lean transformation—which had the twin curses of being both top-down and outside-in—became even more so as its second year unfolded. I felt I was watching a train wreck...or more appropriately, a bus wreck (and praise be to those who showed the good sense not to board the bus without a better idea about where it was heading). My expanding research, which started out of sheer curiosity, increasingly confirmed what I was witnessing. In one article I came upon, John Bernard, CEO of a consulting firm specializing in employee engagement, explained how Lean, which he generally favors, manages to fail:

> "As I looked further into the initiatives, it became obvious that many things were changed, but the changes were window dressing (cosmetic things like simpler forms, making it easier to find things, etc.). Sadly there had been a lot of hard work with nothing to show for it. Following the projects, most employees had little interest in participating in additional future initiatives. This was partly because the work was difficult, but most importantly, the employees could not celebrate a clear, fact-based

victory. The work lacked both extrinsic and intrinsic reward.

"This example only addresses part of the problem in jumping onto the latest management-technique bandwagon. Again and again, I have seen lean manufacturing brought into an organization. It lasts about three years until the zealots finally wear down and acquiesce to the way things have always been done." [xxxiii]

By March, 2013, when I started this book in earnest, an RIE Report Out more than a year into the transformation was still citing employee engagement as a *target* state! Yet the completion plan for that Report Out contained the following items:

1. Fill out Project In-Take Form for Proposed Project Operations Framework Model
2. Create a mock up of a mega board on the wall
3. Add explanation to what and how boards will work
4. Research possible material to use for boards, cards, etc.

There were due dates and people assigned for the completion of these tasks, but not a single item devoted to employee engagement...not a word about achieving the employee buy-in that was so essential to the effort yet had proven so elusive. As it became increasingly clear to me that WE was on a path much like the one John Bernard describes above, I had to decide if I would take my witness public or stifle it and let WTF continue unchallenged to impose its process-over-people culture on WE over the next three years.

THE EMPEROR'S NEW CLOTHES

So off went the Emperor in procession under his splendid canopy. Everyone in the streets and the windows said, "Oh, how fine are the Emperor's new clothes! Don't they fit him to perfection? And see his long train!" Nobody would confess that he couldn't see anything, for that would prove him either unfit for his position, or a fool.

"But he hasn't got anything on," said a little child.

"Did you ever hear such innocent prattle?" asked its father. And then one person whispered to another what the child had said, "He hasn't anything on. A child says he hasn't anything on."

"But he hasn't got anything on!" the whole town cried out at last.

The Emperor shivered, for he suspected they were right. But he thought, "This procession has got to go on." So he walked more proudly than ever, as his noblemen held high the train that wasn't there at all.

"The Emperor's New Clothes" may be the greatest story in children's literature because it so sharply cuts to a dilemma at the heart of a very serious and perplexing adult situation. That is, what to do when you perceive something's going wrong at a station or two above you? Do you, as they say, "know your place" and keep your mouth shut, or do you declaim for moral, legal or practical reasons your dissent from the conventional wisdom? Daniel Ellsburg, Karen Silkwood, Erin Brockovich, Jeffrey Wigand, Wendell Potter, Edward Snowden...the roster of people who have stepped forward to blow the whistle on authority has made for some of the most compelling drama of our times. It is so because the line between whistle blowing and sabotage is a murky one. Who it is that's ultimately motivated to speak truth to power makes for fascinating character study. Are these people so full of character that they can no longer abide the injustice and/or criminality they observe, or are they so devoid of character that betrayal of those who have taken them into their confidence is unalloyed perfidy?

What I am doing here with this book is neither as noble nor traitorous as the actions of various presumed whistleblowers. The stakes are nowhere near as high as, say, they were for Karen Silkwood or Jeffrey Wigand who were calling attention to life threatening acts by their employers. My employer, WE, threatens neither lives nor even business integrity. As far as I know, the same could be said of WTF, however much that company has emerged as the villain of this piece. This is not an indictment of criminality or corruption. As it happens, I wrote the script for our company's video on its ethical standards, so I'm rather familiar with WE's standards and policies on the subject and can say without hesitation that they are comprehensive and genuine.

Still, there are common elements that run through all our stories of individuals—from the child in "The Emperor's New Clothes" to Bradley Manning in today's headlines—who dare to call out, "Wait! What's wrong with this picture?" There's the loneliness of it, at least at first. There's dealing with the charge of betrayal. There's the very high threshold of providing a burden of proof, sometimes via purloined documents. There's the resentment of would-be beneficiaries, co-workers who see challenges to workplace safety or legality as threats of a workplace shut down.

Yet, as the script I did for our company's ethics video makes clear, the company vitally depends upon employees coming forth with reports of wrongdoing or negligence. And Lean famously includes among its core practices employee empowerment to "stop the line." That is, when problems of quality, safety or efficiency appear along the assembly line, each employee is encouraged to flip a switch to stop the line so the problem can be addressed immediately.

Unfortunately the practice did not extend to Lean itself, at least as WTF did it. If it had, someone somewhere along the line would've asked 5 whys on why gaining employee buy-in had proven so elusive (and "change is hard" would have been disqualified as the answer to any of the *whys*). Someone would have challenged the practicality or advisability of restricting "thinking" to A3-sized paper because that's the way it was done back in the day at Toyota. Someone would have suggested doing a 6S to eliminate the waste in WTF's processes.

Whether an outside consultancy group ever allows its expertise to be challenged, I'd guess, would depend upon the self-confidence of the consultants, how highly and genuinely they value collaboration, and what the client company has written into the consultancy agreement. I'd say if questioning authority is a company value, then that should definitely be part of the original agreement. I have acted on the belief that questioning authority is part of WE's values. I feel rather confident in that belief by a page on our intranet where, under the heading "Guiding Company Values," appeared the following quotation from Mahatma Gandhi: "A No uttered from the deepest conviction is better than a Yes merely uttered to please, or worse, to avoid trouble."

I'm proud to have worked for a company bold enough to put forth that statement as a guiding principle. Although it's clear from the existence of this book, I'm disappointed in how WE seemingly sacrificed that aspect of our culture to WTF's agenda for changing that culture. From the company's standpoint, it seriously muddies the message you're trying to send to employees about stepping forward if they witness ethically questionable activity that could harm the company.

I further wonder how this ambiguity may have played a part in Toyota's recall problems. When a company plays as large a role as Toyota does in Japan's economy, there must be tremendous pressure, both political and commercial, to keep things running smoothly, to the point of ignoring problems and not stopping the line. The same goes for the South American Toyota factories, which have received the closest scrutiny for Toyota's troubles. Those factories represent precious new sources of income for both the local governments and the workers. How does a company create an atmosphere where workers understand the importance of raising a critical voice without being destructive? I fully appreciate how difficult it must be for a company's management to navigate between encouraging input from its employees yet guarding against input that turns negative and gets counter-productive. At the cost of dragging another automotive company in on this, I'd say that getting clarity and common understanding on that question should be *job one*.

Ground rules that cut both ways are essential— the company promises no reprisals for honest criticism; the employee promises to keep criticism within the process and out of the gossip pool. One would think that after centuries of worker-management relations some real progress would have been made in this direction, yet employers persist on taking their chances with employee unhappiness. Part of that, I believe, is due to the fact that employers have a limited view of how workers can and do express their dissatisfaction. They know (and fear) unionization and strikes. And they know the "take-this-job-and-shove-it" approach is more satisfying as a C&W song than it is as an actual job action.

Workers, however, have so many more means of expressing dissatisfaction than management can ever imagine or ever be able to eliminate completely. One of my favorite examples comes from Nassim Nicholas Taleb's book, *The Black Swan: The Impact of the Highly Improbable*, where he tells the tale of an investment trader (Nero) who held the annual company review in contempt because it was rigged to force employees to strive for short-term profits at the risk of causing long-term harm to both the investors and the financial system at large. Taleb writes:

> "Nero sat down and listened very calmly
> to the evaluation of his 'supervisor.'
> When Nero was handed the evaluation
> form, he tore it into small pieces in front
> of him. He did this very slowly,
> accentuating the contrast between the
> nature of the act and the tranquility with

which he tore the paper. The boss watched him blank with fear, eyes popping out of his head. Nero focused on his undramatic slow-motion act, elated by both the feeling of standing up for his beliefs and the aesthetics of its execution. The combination of elegance and dignity was exhilarating. He knew that he would either be fired or left alone. He was left alone." xxxiv

Years before my employment at WE, I was a public school teacher in a system where we were contractually allowed 10 sick days a year. Days that weren't used were rolled over until the next year, and it was possible for a teacher at retirement to collect a check for all unused sick days. One year there was a turnover on the board of education in favor of a clique that made public cause of cracking down on what they viewed as teachers' excessive benefits. So they rewrote the contract to make the sick days' provision a "use-them-or-lose-them" proposition. Suddenly veteran teachers who had been reluctant to take days off for numerous reasons and were happy to view their accumulated sick days as part of their retirement package started phoning in sick in unprecedented numbers. The school district went into a panic trying to find enough substitute teachers to cover absented classrooms. And of course rather than having all the accumulated unused sick pay at their disposal for investing until the teachers cashed in at retirement, the board had to bust their budget to pay for substitutes.

At another stop in my career on my way to WE, I again worked in a creative department, which was tucked away well out of public view. Thus we were allowed relative freedom in regards to dress, meaning the guys didn't have to wear ties—until one day someone up the chain of command decided for the sake of a standardized corporate image we did have to wear ties. As it happened, this new directive came down just as we were preparing collateral materials for the company's biggest event of the year. One of our production artists, someone WTF would label an artisan or craft, took exception to the must-wear-ties rule and refused to put one on. The first day he received a warning. The second day he received a warning. On the third day he was told that if he came in the next without a tie, he would be fired. He came in without a tie, but before they could alert HR and summon security to escort him out of the building, he took a scissors and an X-acto knife to the two weeks' worth of work he had created for the great annual corporate event. So two days before the event, the company had to scramble to bring in free lancers to recreate his work. Being free-lancers, of course, they arrived not wearing ties.

I mention these incidents because they're close to the outer boundaries of passive and aggressive employee resistance to company policies. On the extreme end of aggressiveness, of course, we have what unfortunately became popularly known as "going postal." On the extreme end of the passive response is resignation, sometimes expressed in the one devastatingly dismissive word "Whatever." Then there's always the passive/aggressive smile to the corporate face combined with the roll of the eyes behind the corporate back. It may be the most typical way employees express dissatisfaction. It's certainly the easiest and most risk free, and thus it became commonplace among staff during our Lean transformation...far more common than writing a book.

One of the most surprising observations for me during that period was how much stock management chose to put in the smiles and how oblivious they seemed to the eye-roll. The great Paul Simon line comes to mind: "Still a man hears what he wants to hear and disregards the rest." Management, generally, also seems to have an exaggerated faith in how much they can control outright staff communication through memos, indirection, and threat. Turning a deaf ear or blind eye to employee discontent or ordering employees to stifle themselves are not only ineffective, but are counterproductive in that such measures only add to employee disgruntlement.

Yet, amazingly, this seems to be part of the Lean *modus operandi*, all hosannas about respecting people to the contrary. George Koenigsaecker, author of *Leading the Lean Enterprise Transformation*, serves as a senior vice president and board member of Simpler, one of those industrial-sized Lean consulting firms that spans the globe. He gave an interview in which he was quite open about the process-over-people mentality that drives Lean:

Interviewer: What is the most difficult aspect of managing a conversion?

Koenigsaecker: Ohno talked about an organization being like the human body and that a human body is designed to be self-protective. There are antibodies inside the body. When a foreign substance enters the body—an infection—the antibodies not only get more active they also multiply. Ohno says an organization operates the same way. The antibodies create a company's culture. The stronger the culture, the stronger the antibodies because they define what a company will do and also what it won't do.

When you start a conversion like this, you're redefining your company culture in terms of what you will and won't do. The people who are the most loyal members who you know love the company will be some of the biggest resisters of the process because they are trying to protect the company as it has been as opposed to how the company will be. You need to actively address that

group or their efforts to protect the
corporate culture will defeat any effort
to change the culture in a way that will
allow you to become a lean enterprise.

Interviewer: Do you need hard-ass
managers to make it happen?

Koenigsaecker: When you start in a
new organization, one way or another,
you have to make sure that everyone in
the organization and especially the
antibodies know that their choice is to
join up with this new way or find a
different organization. Most managers
are very much afraid of making that
decision. There are not many people
willing to do that. [xxxv]

The two men who were primarily responsible
for the success of ThedaCare, Roger Gerard and John
S. Toussaint, wrote a book about it called *On the
Mend.* On the acknowledgements page of their book
Koenigsaecker comes in for special recognition as a
valued mentor to their transformation. I don't doubt
the sincerity of their debt to the man. Gerard and
Toussaint strike me as honorable men. But one

wonders how someone walks into a hospital environment uttering such rank nonsense about "antibodies" without being laughed out of the place. As I've said, we're all entitled to our own metaphors, but we're also responsible for the implications of them. The implication of this one is clear: Lean is an infection and people who love the company and are most loyal to it are the problem!

Taken in conjunction with Ohno-san's injunction against listening to veterans, it imposes upon management committed to a Lean transformation a mandate to do battle against what should be some of its most valued employees. I suspect this was not an issue at ThedaCare because either Koenigsaecker was a good enough salesman not to try and warn doctors about the perils of antibodies—or more likely, that doctors, rare in numbers and skills (like star athletes and software developers), get deferential treatment. Gerard and Toussaint, in fact, say they had to spend the first year of their Lean transformation *proving* to their medical staff the value of Lean. "One of our biggest mistakes was that we didn't answer the question: *What's in it for me...*I mean for our doctors and nurses," says

Toussaint. There's a world of difference between having to provide a burden of proof and just having to provide a one-way ticket on the bus to the unemployment line.

In any case, unlike "respect for people," the principle of distrust your best people did not make it on to any of WTF's slide presentations. On the other hand, unlike respect for people it permeated the workplace to the point where it ultimately depressed morale. That alone would be bad enough, but it sets Lean against itself. How do you call for continuous improvement, how do you encourage "stopping the line" when your overriding message is go along or get out? Again, this seems to be an internal contradiction at the core of Lean that its proponents, WTF and others, just gloss over.

At the time of the push to our open floor plan, when fresh research was making plain the error of it, or at least raising sobering questions about it, there was a lengthy article in *The New Yorker* debunking the value of Alex Osborn's brainstorming approach to problem solving. Charlan Nemeth, professor of psychology at Cal Berkeley, conducted extensive studies that exposed one of the key myths about brainstorming. In its formalized state, as outlined in his 1948 book, *Your Creative Power*, Osborn places great emphasis on congenial personalities and discourages challenging personalities. But the new research shows the more contentious participants are more valuable than accommodators who feel an overwhelming need to push for collegiality and consensus. Jonah Lehrer writes in *The New Yorker*:

> "Nemeth's studies suggest that the ineffectiveness of brainstorming stems from the very thing that Osborn thought was most important. As Nemeth puts it, 'While the instruction 'Do not criticize' is often cited as the important instruction in brainstorming, this appears to be a counterproductive strategy. Our findings show that debate and criticism do not inhibit ideas but, rather, stimulate them relative to every other condition.' Osborn thought that imagination is inhibited by the merest hint of criticism, but Nemeth's work and a number of other studies have demonstrated that it can thrive on conflict.

"According to Nemeth, dissent stimulates new ideas because it encourages us to engage more fully with the work of others and to reassess our viewpoints. 'There's this Pollyannaish notion that the most important thing to do when working together is stay positive and get along, to not hurt anyone's feelings,' she says. 'Well, that's just wrong. Maybe debate is going to be less pleasant, but it will always be more productive. True creativity requires some trade-offs.'" xxxvi

WTF's entire approach placed an onerous premium on accommodation to its particular vision at the cost of honest skepticism about its ways and means and their appropriateness for our company, thus depriving the company of the opportunity to achieve credible, fully vetted resolutions. Furthermore that approach put WTF at cross-purposes with its goal of helping us achieve a state of continuous improvement. Continuous improvement depends upon constant critiquing more than it does on consensus.

In *Thinking, Fast and Slow*, Kahneman draws upon his own empirical observations to bring home to corporate leaders the need to hear rather than eliminate dissenting voices. He says that the closing of the corporate mind to criticism places the company at risk, and though this closing may sometimes be unconscious and unavoidable, there is an opening. He writes:

> "The voice of reason may be fainter than the loud and clear voice of an erroneous intuition, and questioning your intuitions is unpleasant when you face the stress of a big decision. More doubt is the last thing you want when you are in trouble. The upshot is that it is much easier to identify a minefield when you observe others wandering into it than when you are about to do so. Observers are less cognitively busy and more open to information than actors." [xxxvii]

In short, every emperor needs a little boy, or an adult at least, willing to see the new outfit for what it is...or more importantly what it isn't.

STONE SOUP

Once upon a time, a Lean consultant wandered into a company where the employees had stopped eating lunch because their dining area created such a hodgepodge of odors that drifted into the work place that no one had an appetite for food. The Lean consultant said, "I have the answer. We'll feed everyone a harmonious stone soup." No one had ever heard of stone soup, but they all eagerly gathered around the break room hot plate as the Lean consultant dropped a stone into a pot of boiling water. The Lean consultant leaned over the pot and smelled the broth and licked his lips in anticipation, and said, "Stone soup always goes better with oregano." And just like that the resourceful department manager went to his briefcase and broke out a kilo of oregano (or something like oregano). The Lean consultant added the spice, sniffed the soup, and sighed, "So much better, but what a feast we'd have with a carrot." And just then the resident vegan jumped up and pulled a carrot out of her purse and added it to the soup. Anticipation in the room grew as the Lean consultant bent in for another whiff. "Gosh, all it really needs now is a chicken leg," he proclaimed. "Whoa, I have a chicken leg in my drawer!" shouted the ambitious new hire. And the leg was added to the soup. Soon all the once hungry workers were dining on the finest soup they ever ate and paid the Lean consultant handsomely for teaching them how to make such splendid stone soup.

Let me restate something important here at the beginning of the end of this cautionary tale: I am not anti-Lean. I've seen and read enough about Lean in my personal Lean journey to appreciate its benefits. I do feel, however, that it is grossly oversold by its most zealous proponents and projects cult-like aspects that are off-putting to people who are more concerned with doing their jobs well and earning a living than they are with validating anyone's pet methodology.

I would restate a few other things about Lean that I may have stated too obliquely in the course of this book. So for the sake of utmost clarity, let me serve them up again here in a delectable soup of treasured stones.

Emerald: Stay within yourself. I would say that the whole idea of a company turning itself over to another company for a total culture makeover is a very bad idea regardless of the methodology the consultants are selling. Employees, especially the managerial class, the veterans, the experts in a particular field are automatically and rightly suspicious of outsiders coming in and telling them how to do their jobs. Corporate history is littered with examples of how badly this works out. It's a verity that should be as obvious to any corporate head as the need to answer to the bottom line. How and why any company leader comes to believe that outsiders—whose real abilities rather than résumé abilities remain untested—will be welcome with open arms by tried and trusted employees is one of the great mysteries of the corporate mind. Even more mysterious is that any corporate head thinks the way around this problem is to order employees to embrace the consultants. The ultimate effect of this is not to foster acceptance, but resentment.

Lean practitioners believe the way around this problem is to make a preemptive attack on the dissenters, warning upper management that its vision for improvement through Lean will be put at risk by listening to those most knowledgeable and loyal to the company. Nice work if you can get it. I would say that if, as a corporate head, you have concluded that to remake your company culture you have to turn the keys of your company over to an outside company, you should be thinking about retiring or selling. There really should be a limit to outsourcing, and I'd say handing your company culture over to others to mold for you is it. Better to spend your company's money and your employees' time engaged in a corporate-wide self-examination, clearly identifying your company culture, critiquing it, and refining it for the future. Call in outside help as you and your people need it...and know precisely why and where you need it.

Pearl: Don't try to boil the ocean. At their Harvard Business Review Blog, Michael Zinser and David Ryeson write:

> "One of the most common mistakes... when embarking on a lean program is trying to do too much at once. These 'boil the ocean' initiatives are long, costly and often end up stalling under the weight of their own ambition." xxxviii

With shareholders, investors, market watchers and the like becoming more and more like children with ADD every year, the pressure for corporate leaders to quickly deliver huge returns grows exponentially, forcing them to attempt bigger changes at bigger risks. Gradual, incremental changes would seem to be the most prudent strategy, especially if you're trying to implement a methodology reputedly built on "continuous improvement" as Lean is. They don't call it "all-at-once improvement," so why introduce it all at once? In *What About Bob?* the psychologist played by Richard Dreyfuss introduces his totally dysfunctional client played by Bill Murray to his patented therapy called "Baby Steps." Dreyfuss's character counsels that it's better to address one's problems incrementally, building on small successes. Comedy or not, this seems to be a far more rational approach than attempting to address complex and far-flung global problems with one big bang. This is not an alien notion to Lean. I've read Lean bloggers and on my tour witnessed Lean practitioners talk in terms of small wins. The small wins not only start to move the company forward in the desired direction, but they help build staff confidence in and understanding of the methods the company is trying to instill. The attempt at a massive transformation only serves to send one of two messages to the people on the factory floor: One is that the consultant bamboozled the client into overbuying; two is that the client, the corporate head, is desperate.

Ruby: It's lonely at the top. Daniel Kahneman, who has spent decades studying corporate leaders and working through their problems with them, is quite sensitive to the decision-making they often have to make in isolation. That's why he spends so much time in *Thinking, Fast and Slow* counseling corporate leaders against fear, which they often try to mask with their own swagger. Either the fear or the swagger meant to cloak it, both have a chilling effect on honest feedback from staff thereby limiting a chief executive's access to diverse viewpoints and ultimately increasing the isolation factor. He writes:

> "As a team converges on a decision and especially when the leader tips her hand public doubts about the wisdom of the planned move are gradually suppressed and eventually come to be treated as evidence of flawed loyalty to the team and its leaders. The suppression of doubt contributes to overconfidence in a group where only supporters of the decision have a voice." [xxxix]

Kahneman offers as one small antidote to this problem a suggestion made by Gary Klein, who he describes as a chief protagonist of his, thus demonstrating Kahneman's willingness to walk the talk and listen to divergent voices. Klein puts forth the idea of a "pre-mortem." In the pre-mortem the corporate head gathers together all the key people involved in making a company decision before this decision is implemented and tells them to imagine a year down the line when the decision just made has proved to be a disaster. The chief exec then asks everyone to take 5-10 minutes to write a brief history of that disaster and what made it happen. Klein and Kahneman believe that this simple act frees people up to think more critically and feel safer voicing their criticisms.

I would further suggest that corporate heads make a point of assigning a Vice President of Devil's Advocacy. Perhaps it can be a rotating position so no one person feels at a career disadvantage by being forced into the role of company contrarian. In any case, one person should be directed to not only argue against any proposed idea, but to support the argument with outside research. Such a procedure would help create a comfort level for corporate leaders in accepting criticism and for subordinates in offering it. Plus it would send a healthy message to staff at large that the company values and practices constructive criticism.

In a paper that examines Lean implementation failures, Christopher Schlichting pinpoints failure of leadership by upper-management as the primary cause. [xl] (The secondary cause, he says, is failure to engage employees.) I would argue that the pressure Lean brings to bear on leaders to make the Lean implementation work is the root cause of the problem, and I believe if Lean practitioners asked themselves 5 honest whys on the subject they would come to the same conclusion. The demands of a standard work schedule alone are totally unrealistic for company leaders with heavy portfolios and broad range of commitments. Add to that the obligation to do battle with core staff if they resist Lean. That's burden enough for a corporate leader asked to go all in for a methodology with a success rate that is, for all the massaging, anemic. It is no wonder that so many corporate leaders bail on their Lean commitment. It's not for lack of commitment to Lean, it is because of the realization that Lean cannot become the company's *raison d'être* no matter how much its proponents insist that it be. If Lean unfolds as it has unfolded at WE, at some point a leader must ask: Is my primary goal here to make Lean work optimally or to make my company work optimally? The two goals may actually be in conflict.

Sapphire: Success is not fungible...or not as much as Lean people may think it is. My favorite National Football League team is the New England Patriots. Before 2001, the Patriots spent much of their history as a laughingstock of the NFL. With new management instituting something that would become known as The Patriot Way, the Pats went on to enjoy more than a decade of unprecedented success. Midway through that success, one of the architects of it, Scott Pioli, twice NFL Executive of the Year, was lured away from New England to duplicate The Patriot Way with the Kansas City Chiefs. Pioli brought a coach, a quarterback, and a defensive player intended to bring a championship attitude into the Chief's locker room. Pioli also brought with him standards he had helped devise on evaluation and development of Patriot players as well as the Patriot business model, which had been highly praised by the Harvard School of Business. Without bogging this book down in the details, the Patriot business model consisted of, among other things, not hanging onto favorite veterans for sentimental reasons, signing as many players with multiple skill sets as possible to maximize interchangeability, and spreading the league-wide salary cap number more evenly among mid-range players rather than tying up too much in a few superstars. (And, yes, I'm aware that there are a few overlaps with Lean in that approach.)

By his second season, Pioli had guided the Chiefs to their first playoff win in years, and it looked like The Patriot Way was indeed transferable. But the Chiefs declined precipitously over the next two seasons on the field. And off the field more than half the pre-Pioli staff had resigned, and the fan base—once known for its rabid loyalty—turned against the team and took to wearing black arm bands to home games. The Patriot Way had not taken in Kansas City, and Pioli was suddenly out of his job.

Kahneman reiterates with example after example that executives get too much credit or too much blame for the fortunes of the companies they've been hired to run. As with most of his findings he uses lots of data accumulated over many years to support his contention that most executives, including the so-called superstar executives, are the windsocks of chance...luck, good or bad, usually has more to say about their legacies than talent. In Pioli's case, it may not be coincidence that his first two Executive of the Year Awards came when he had the doubly good fortune of working with a hall of fame quarterback and a hall of fame head coach.

How sure can we ever be that methods that prove successful in one environment will transfer with equal success to another, especially with luck always as a key variable? Here's an excerpt from Mark Graban's review of Gerard and Toussaint's *On the Mend*, interestingly titled, "Read This Book, But Don't Copy ThedaCare":

> "In my plea to not copy ThedaCare, I mean no disrespect to the work they've done. Far from it. What I mean is a cautionary statement...that there 'is no instant pudding,' as Dr. W. Edwards Deming once said. Too many organizations want a simple roadmap – they want to copy... They want to

implement Lean without having to think...

"What's great about ThedaCare's story is that they learned from others and they didn't copy directly. They learned from Wisconsin manufacturers. They learned from general Lean books... they innovated and used PDCA to refine their process designs...they didn't blindly copy...." [xli]

I would say that the instinct to copy someone else's success is the trap both my company and the Kansas City Chiefs fell into, so it transcends Lean. It is a trap set by looking only at the results of someone else's formula or "way" of doing things, and not at the hard, trial and error process (and luck) that went into producing that particular "way." If slavishly following someone else's blueprint was all there was to it, every auto manufacturer could have duplicated Toyota's success; every hospital, ThedaCare's; every football team, the Patriots. But every organization is different in myriad ways—from location, to employee pool, to industry demands and idiosyncrasies, to culture, etc. The real secret sauce in the making of a winning organization is what went into making it so...what did it learn about itself along the way. That kind of wisdom is simply not transferable. It may not even be knowable to the companies that have gone through it because nothing gets forgotten quicker than wrong turns along the way.

In an interview, Michael Ballé says,

> "Lean gives you an ideal; it's a commitment to an ideal. More importantly, you must understand your own organization, the culture that exists ...You have to rid yourself of Lean or other business processes...If you are successful at implementing Lean, it is simply not Lean. It's yours." [xlii]

I love the implied Buddhism of that statement...the whole idea that when Lean is most effective is when it disappears into your culture (not replaces your culture). Unfortunately, when Lean arrives at your company doorstep with all the subtlety of an invading army intent on shock and awe that pretty much forecloses the possibility of ever achieving that ideal.

Topaz: Stay humble. There's need for very much more humility from Lean. There's evidence of it here and there, as in Ballé's statement, but it was totally missing in WTF's approach to WE, and I suspect that's the rule rather than exception. Lean is really quite too full of itself these days. For example, ThedaCare's Lean transformation legend is based on outcomes such as this: the mortality rate for coronary bypass surgery dropped there from 4% a year (12 deaths) to almost zero (one death in 2009). As one Lean zealot wrote in reporting on this statistic: "These kind of results are attributed to the application of the principles of the Toyota Production System (TPS)."

That's terrific all the way around—for the hospital, for the patients, for Lean. But there's a serious problem when Lean advocates make it seem as if such positive outcomes are only possible through Lean. At the same time ThedaCare was going through its arduous (and I daresay expensive) Lean transformation, other hospitals in the US were experimenting with a simple checklist for medical staff to standardize work. Modeled after the checklist airline pilots must go through before take-off, the results were easily as impressive as ThedaCare's Lean results. The following is from a New York Times review of Atul Gawande's book *The Checklist Manifesto*:

> "...A five-point checklist implemented in 2001 virtually eradicated central line infections in the intensive care unit at Johns Hopkins Hospital, preventing an estimated 43 infections and eight deaths over 27 months. Gawande notes that when it was later tested in I.C.U.'s in Michigan, the checklist decreased infections by 66 percent within three months and probably saved more than 1,500 lives within a year and a half." [xliii]

Back to *Thinking Fast and Slow* where Kahneman tells the story of an anesthesiologist named Virginia Apgar who made a major contribution to reducing infant mortality in the US. One morning over breakfast she was pondering what she would do about the problem and jotted down five vital signs to watch for. Then she applied values to each sign. That helped her produce an algorithm that proved reliable over time—an infant that scored 8 or above on her scale was safe; one that scored 4 or below was at risk;

in between warranted watching. This was in 1953 before TPS had hardly become a system at all and was still safely confined to the Toyota factory floor in Japan.

Dan Markovitz, Shingo Award Winning author of the book *A Factory of One: Applying Lean Principles to Banish Waste and Improve Your Personal Performance,* takes strong issue with a recent *Fortune* magazine article that rang the death knell for Lean. The article focused on troubles other Asian companies practicing Lean were experiencing, and Markovitz struck back as follows:

> "The more significant issue is that kaizen isn't the Japanese business model, any more than 'maximizing shareholder value' is the American business model. Further, ascribing Sharp's problems—or Sony's, or Olympus's, or Panasonic's—to the relentless pursuit of quality, without considering other factors such as leadership, the rising yen, cultural insularity, etc. is absurd. I'm surprised that article didn't trot out the hoary

fallacy that just-in-time production has caused the downfall of these electronics giants." [xliv]

To which I say: Amen to that, brother. To contend that Lean is responsible for the troubles of all these companies is a gross simplification—as gross as it is to give Lean credit for all their successes. But this is the bed Lean has made for itself and the one it must lie in until it remakes it.

In his book on "the highly improbable," Nassim Nicholas Taleb maintains that people who fail spectacularly oftentimes possess the same qualities as those who succeed spectacularly—courage, risk-taking, optimism. The only difference is that the latter choose to tell their stories. "...People who fail do not seem to write memoirs," says Taleb. Nor do companies, it seems. In Christopher Schlichting's study of Lean transformations that failed, he found the biggest obstacle to his research was that companies are not very forthcoming when things go wrong. (In that regard, this book seeks to be a corrective in a small way, at least in terms of WE, for the benefit of researchers everywhere.)

I'm from the "Whatever Works" school of thought. You're welcome to the "My Way or the Highway" school if you can afford the isolation, ignorance and ill will that comes with it.

Jade: Physician, heal thyself. Stop blaming managers and antibodies when your process fails! People will trump process most every time. Lex Schroeder from LEI disagrees. She writes:

> "...nine times out of 10 problems have to do with processes, not people... unless we're talking about people's <u>capability</u> for solving problems. Lean practitioners have found this to be true at organizations of all different stripes... Good lean consultants help people design better problem-solving processes and improve their management <u>systems</u> in order to help people focus more attention on solving problems rather than blaming people." [xlv]

As with so much from LEI, the intentions are good. They want managers to focus on clearing a path so their workers can work under optimal conditions. But, also, like so much from LEI, it's almost hopelessly naive. The perspective that 90% of workplace issues can be traced to process, not people, can only be held by someone who has spent too much time observing workplaces rather than actually working in one.

This cuts directly, I'd say, to why failure to engage employees registers as so high a factor in Lean's sorry 2% rate in sustaining itself at companies after its initial launch. Lean practitioners simply underestimate how big a factor personality is and how much work it requires to navigate through human diversity because they have an inflated view of their process. I think this is a fundamental problem because the people most attracted to Lean in the first place are those most enamored of process and far less interested in how people are wired and the play of human dynamics. This is as natural a state to the Lean practitioner as, say, working alone is to the artisan. And I don't know that it's any more fair or reasonable to expect the Lean practitioner to suddenly "get people" than it is to expect the artisan to suddenly "get working in a group."

The Lean advocate truly believes that the process is a benign great leveler. But for over a year I watched up close how personalities manipulated the process to suit their own needs. The process could not make a harmony out of the power-hungry, the fearful, the Pollyannas, the embittered. Each, in that incredibly clever human way we humans have, found a way to ride the process to whatever he or she wanted...more power, more fear, greater optimism, deeper resentment. People use tools as befits their own biases, tendencies, and goals. No process will make a bad manager good or a weak manager strong...or anybody at all more responsive to the process rather than their own personality—unless that personality consists of an overweening affection for process.

Common sense tells us that we are made of diverse personalities, and the work environment functions best when personalities can be made to bend and blend, rather than conform to a rigid and artificial model. Every process works to the extent that human beings understand it, accept it and allow it to work. Lean is at best a set of tools for helping people do their jobs better. It is not, nor should it even try to be, a tool for changing human behavior. That is simply beyond the scope of its analytics and the skill-set of its agents.

Diamond: Keep it simple. W. Edwards Deming famously had his 7 deadly diseases for businesses. So in his honor I will limit my soup here to 7 treasured stones. And I'll dedicate this last one to the great man himself. I agree with those Lean thinkers who believe that Deming was a great man based on his monumental work in helping post-war Japan rise from the ashes, as well as his 14 Principles, which came out of that effort and which I believe have real and lasting value to all businesses regardless of time and place. Those principles are always worth revisiting when the subject is business transformation. So it seems especially pertinent as I approach the end of this book to review them. Herewith, Deming's 14 Principles:

> 1. Create constancy of purpose towards improvement of product and service, with the aim to become competitive, stay in business, and to provide jobs.
> 2. Adopt the new philosophy. We are in a new economic age. Western management must awaken to the

challenge, must learn their responsibilities, and take on leadership for change.

3. Cease dependence on inspection to achieve quality. Eliminate the need for inspection on a mass basis by creating quality into the product in the first place.

4. End the practice of awarding business on the basis of price tag. Instead minimize total cost. Move towards a single supplier for any one item, on a long-term relationship of loyalty and trust.

5. Improve constantly and forever the system of production and service, to improve quality and productivity, and thus constantly decrease costs.

6. Institute training on the job.

7. Institute leadership (sec point 12). The aim of leadership should be to help people and machines and gadgets to do a better job. Leadership of management

is in need of overhaul, as well as leadership of production workers.

8. Drive out fear so that everyone may work effectively for the company.

9. Break down barriers between departments. People in research, design, sales, and production must work as a team, to foresee problems of production and in use that may be encountered with the product or service.

10. Eliminate slogans, exhortations, and targets for the work force that ask for zero defects and new levels of productivity.

11a. Eliminate work standards (quotas) on the factory floor. Substitute leadership.

11b. Eliminate management by objective. Eliminate management by numbers, numerical goals. Substitute leadership.

12a. Remove barriers that rob the hourly worker of his right to pride of workmanship. The responsibility of supervisors must be changed from sheer numbers to quality.

12b. Remove barriers that rob people in management and in engineering of their right to pride in workmanship. This means inter alia, abolishment of the annual or merit rating and of management by objective, management by the numbers

13. Institute a vigorous program of education and self-improvement.

14. Put everybody in the company to work to accomplish the transformation. The transformation is everybody's job.

Now at various points throughout this book I've taken issue with one or two of those items. Regardless, here's why I choose to highlight all the principles here at the end: They are clear and simple. They are stated in such a way that most any employee can understand them and most any manager can use them as a guide in leading a productive discussion about company culture and goals with staff. It brings tears to my eyes just thinking how much better off my company would be if—rather than WTF—managers, skilled or trained in leading group discussions, had met with employees once a week to conduct conversations around each of those principles in turn. For example, the manager throws this up on the big screen or white board:

> Create constancy of purpose toward improvement of product and service, with the aim to become competitive, stay in business and to provide jobs.

Then the manager addresses staff: Okay, group, what do you think of this as a principle in general? What are your thoughts about our product? Where do you think we could improve our product? What would you be willing to do to improve it? Who's our competition? What do you think of our competition? What does our competition do better than we do? What do you think we can do to compete better? Does competition worry you? Does our competition present any risk to you personally? Have you ever worked for our competition or known anyone who has sampled its products? What was their experience? How important do you think it would be for us as a company to trim benefits to stay competitive? To trim staff to stay competitive? What cuts would you be willing to make to save jobs? What ideas do you have to save the company costs? How do we set and maintain standards for ourselves? What's the one action we should do in the next week as a result of this discussion? How about the next month? The next year?

I maintain that's the kind of thing that can engage employees on a profound level and help build an effective company culture from the inside out. Deming's 14 principles are like The Sermon on the Mount—a great philosophy distilled to its simplest form before the priestly robes, stained glass icons, church hierarchies, A3's, 6S's, the *kaizens* and the whatnot come along to complicate and distort. That's a recipe for a wholesome and hearty stone soup that employees can and will cook up for their company if given half the chance.

One of the most appealing things for me personally when Lean first arrived at my work place was WTF's reference (in its otherwise sorry orientation PowerPoint) to the Socratic method. As a one-time educator, I fell in love with Socrates' approach to teaching by constantly probing the student with questions aimed at driving thinking deeper and deeper. I've practiced the Socratic method and believed in it...without making a fetish of it...for my entire professional life. Like so much else, WTF managed to muck up the Socratic method by tying it to its simpleminded "5 Whys," the result being a kind of Socratic method for real dummies. Here's an example of how WTF chose to illustrate its "5 Whys":

Problem Statement: Lots of bird droppings on the Jefferson Memorial
Why? Birds perching on the roof
Why? To eat the spiders
Why? Spiders there to eat the moths
Why? Moths gather at dusk
Why? Moths attracted by monument's floodlights, which are turned on earlier than lights at other area sites.
Corrective action: Turn floodlights on half hour later than usual.

     See how easy it is? WTF's model inspired me to invent The Socratic Inquiry Drinking Game. It goes like this: every time you answer a *Why*, take a drink. Here goes:
Problem Statement: My horse is too weak to ride
Why? I cannot water my horse

Why? My bucket won't hold water.

Why? It has a hole in it

Why? My horse kicked it

Why? Because he wanted water

Somewhere in the great beyond Socrates is spitting up his hemlock. If you think WTF's "5 Whys" is the path to Socratic thinking, I have a few points off my IQ I'd like to sell you. The whole idea behind Socratic questioning is that you don't know where the questions will lead either you or the student...there is no neat, programmed path to the corrective action. There is, or should be, great uncertainty with that first *Why* for both the teacher and the student. If the teacher already knows the answer to the *Why*, there's no point in asking it. In fact there's great risk in asking it unless you're challenging a student on a given assignment and *testing* rather than asking. But if you're challenging a student on his or her critical thinking, the question must be legitimate, otherwise the student sniffs out the phoniness in the exercise right off and it becomes—at the risk of going Japanese here—pure kabuki.

If you want to teach this kind of probing thinking, you ask your student or worker to ask a real

Why question—something that has been nagging at him or her, like *Why am I not getting satisfaction from my job?* Which might lead to, *What do you want out of your job?* Or *How did you end up here?* (Another important aspect of real questions is that they don't always start with a *Why*). Really asking questions is high risk, but that's what makes it an engaging act. Only in being willing to take that risk are you able to demonstrate the richness and rewards of the process.

I dwell on this here at the end because this book began with a *Why* question: Why did my company (and so many others) buy into a journey where 90% of the participants quit? If WTF chose to tackle this question, this is how I imagine their PowerPoint slide on it might read:

Problem Statement: Lots of companies sign up for Lean, but lots drop out

Why? Managers give up

Why? Because they're weak-willed, unfocused and lack discipline

Why? Because they were raised that way

Why? Their parents spoiled them

Why? Because their parents were weak-willed, unfocused, and lacked discipline

Corrective action: Get better parents

Here's how my PowerPoint slide might handle the same problem:

Problem Statement: Lots of companies drop in to Lean, but lots drop out.

Why? Managers give up

Why? Because Lean reveals itself as not worth it

Why? Too much emphasis on process

Why? Lean not equipped to deal with people issues

Why? Lean too wedded to manufacturing where process is easier to invoke

Corrective action: Lean stops overselling itself to management as a one-size-fits-all business solution.

Well, that's just my take. I'm sure the true Lean community can do a more thorough job of answering the question. If they believe and care about their methodology, they will take up James Womack's call and start a self-examination immediately before Lean's reputation and time runs out.

As I came to the end of my career at WE, it became increasingly clear that its 5-year Lean initiative would not last beyond three years. Employee engagement remained weak. Multiple middle managers—the praetorian guard of any company—began using such terms as "cult," "brainwashing" and "Gestapo tactics" in discussing WTF Lean. And the most critical blow—the sudden and shocking resignation of our company president and Lean's champion. As a result, Lean events were put on indefinite hold while the company reassessed its commitment. As had happened in so many other places across a broad spectrum of industries where it had planted its flag, Lean had failed to fully engage employees and lost the support of key managers at WE. This failure, I believe, is innate to Lean as long as it remains a *process-over-people* methodology, and can only be remedied by Lean emphatically *reimagining* itself as a process *for* people methodology. If not, it will continue to face a 90% drop out rate...and worse. It will become known for debacles like the one it created at my company where WTF took over WE and through an astounding feat of reverse engineering turned a corporate diamond into a lump of coal.

ENDNOTES

---

[i] Lean is not a proper noun, so it is not normally capitalized. It is merely a conceit of this book that I've capitalized it, except when quoting its use by others.

[ii] Byrne, G, *Principles of Software Flow*, 'Lean's 98+% Failure Rate," November 25, 2010, http://softwareflow.wordpress.com/2010/11/25/debunked-leans-98-failure-rate/

[iii] Fiegerman, S., 'Steve Jobs Would Have Hated What's Happening In The Samsung Patent Trial Right Now', *Business Insider*, August 6, 2012, http://www.businessinsider.com/steve-jobs-would-have-hated-whats-happening-in-the-samsung-patent-trial-right-now-2012-8

[iv] James, G, 'The 8 Stupidest Management Fads of All Time,' *CBS News Moneywatch*, October 12, 2010, http://www.cbsnews.com/8301-505183_162-28552307-10391735/the-8-stupidest-management-fads-of-all-time/

[vi] Levy, P, *Not Running a Hospital*, 'You Don't Do Lean,' July 7, 2012, http://runningahospital.blogspot.com/2012/07/you-dont-do-lean.html

[vii] Kahneman, D, 2011, *Thinking, Fast and Slow*, FSG, p. 87

[viii] Silver, B., *lib.com.org*, '1930-present: Labor unrest and successive geographical restructuring of the world automobile industry,' January, 5, 2010, http://libcom.org/history/1930-present-labour-

unrest-successive-geographical-restructuring-world-automobile-indust

^{ix} Isidore, C., 'Toyota Motors has agreed to pay a record \$17.4 million to the National Highway Traffic Safety Administration for problems that led to a 2012 recall in one of its Lexus models,' *money.cnn.com*, December 12, 2012

^{x} Shook, J, *lean.org*, 'Detroit Auto Show Overshadowed by Dr. Womack's Trashing of Toyota,' January, 25, 2010, http://www.lean.org/shook/DisplayObject.cfm?o=1355

^{xi} Graban, M., *The Lean Blog*, 'The Impact of Toyota's Quality Problems on Lean Healthcare?,' January 30, 2010, http://www.leanblog.org/2010/01/the-impact-of-toyotas-quality-problems-on-lean-healthcare/

^{xii} Spear, S., *The High Veloctiy Edge*, 'Did Toyota Abandon Safety as a Concern?,' May 19, 2010, http://thehighvelocityedge.mhprofessional.com/apps/ab/2010/03/19/did-toyota-abandon-safety-as-a-concern/

^{xiii} Liker, J., *Harvard Business Review Blog*, 'Toyota's Recall Crisis: What Have We Learned?', February 11, 2011

^{xiv} Liker, J., *The Lean Edge*, 'Toyota Recall and The Lean Movement,' January, 30, 2010, http://theleanedge.org/?p=355

^{xv} Womack, J., *lean.org*, 'Beyond Toyota,' January 7, 2010

^{xvi} Byrne, ibid.

^{xvii} Kahneman, ibid., p. 415

xviii Lehrer, J., 'Groupthink: The Brainstorming Myth,' *The New Yorker*, January 30, 2012, http://www.newyorker.com/reporting/2012/01/30/1 20130fa_fact_lehrer

xix Cain, S., 'The Rise of the New Groupthink,' *The New York Times Sunday Review*, January 13, 2012, http://www.nytimes.com/2012/01/15/opinion/sunda y/the-rise-of-the-newgroupthink.html?pagewanted=all&_r=0

xx The Knoll, *The Space Place*, 'The Open Plan versus Enclosed Private Offices: A Review of the Research,' March, 2007, http://www.thespaceplace.net/articles/knoll200703. php

xxi Tierney, J., 'Open Offices Prompting Pleas for Quiet,' *The San Diego Union Tribune*, May 20, 2012, http://www.utsandiego.com/news/2012/may/20/tp-open-offices-prompting-pleas-for-quiet/

xxii Tanaka, M. 'What I Learned from Taiichi Ohno,' *The Birth of Lean*, March, 2009, (The transcript of this talk is available in various places on the web in PDF, including LEI; because download versions will vary, however, I cannot provide exact page numbers for the quotations.)

xxiii Toyota, 'Relations with Employees,' *The Toyota Way*, 2001, http://www.toyota-global.com/sustainability/report/sr/05/pdf/so_02.p df

xxiv Ballé, M., *The Gemba Coach*, 'How Can we Reconcile the Lean Principle of Respect for People with our Disrespectful Atmosphere?,' November 26, 2012 xxv Tanaka, ibid.

xxvi Tanaka, ibid.

xxvii Poppendieck, M., *Lean Software Development*, 'A Tale of Two Terminals,' January 15, 2011, http://www.leanessays.com/2011/01/tale-of-two-terminals.html

xxviii Thrope, G., *Launching Tech Ventures Harvard Business School*, 'Is Lean Flawed? The Case of Aardvark,' February 24, 2013 http://launchingtechventures.blogspot.com/2013/02/is-lean-flawed-case-of-aardvark.html?view=flipcard

xxix Silver, ibid.

xxx Kahneman, ibid., p. 418

xxxi Tanaka, ibid.

xxxii van Ede, J., *Business-Improvement.eu*, 'The Lean Journey of ThedaCare,' October 20, 2010, http://www.businessimprovement.eu/lean/ThedaCare_On_The_Mend.php

xxxiii Bernard, J., 'Why Management Fads Fail,' *Portland Business Journal*, October 22, 2010, http://www.bizjournals.com/portland/print-edition/2010/10/22/why-management-fads-disappoint.html?page=all

xxxiv Taleb, N., *The Black Swan: The Impact of the Highly Improbable*, Random House, 2007, p. 99

xxxv McCormack, R., 'A Manager's Guide to Implementing Lean.' *Manufacturing & Technology News*, May 16, 2001, http://www.manufacturingnews.com/news/01/georgek.html

xxxvi Lehrer, ibid.

xxxvii Kahneman, ibid., p. 417

xxxviii Zinser, M., and Ryeson, D., *HBR Blog Network*, Guidelines for Fast Lean Transformation, March 16, 2011, http://blogs.hbr.org/cs/2011/03/fast_lean_by_michael_zinser.html

xxxix Kahenman, ibid. p. 265

xl Schlichting, C., *Sustaining Lean Improvements*, Master Thesis, December 2009, http://www.wpi.edu/Pubs/ETD/Available/etd-121709-090534/unrestricted/cschlichting.pdf

xli Graban, M., *The Lean Blog*, 'Read—But Don't Copy ThedaCare,' April 27, 2010, http://www.leanblog.org/2010/04/read-this-book-but-dont-copy-thedacare/

xlii *Business 901,* If Less than 1% of companies are successful with Lean,' December 14, 2011, http://business901.com/blog1/if-less-than-1-of-companies-are-successful-with-lean-why-are-we-doing-it/

xliii Jauhar, S., 'One Thing After Another,' *The New York Times*, January 22, 2010, http://www.nytimes.com/2010/01/24/books/review/Jauhar-t.html?_r=0

xliv Markovitz, D., *The Lean Blog*, 'Reports of Kaizen's Death are Greatly Exaggerated,' October 1, 2012, http://www.leanblog.org/2012/10/guest-post-reports-of-kaizens-death-are-greatly-exaggerated/#more-18615

xlv Schroeder, L., *lean.org.*, 'When Problems Arise, What Helps Keep Your Focus on Work?' http://www.lean.org/common/display/?o=2245

www.ingramcontent.com/pod-product-compliance
Lightning Source LLC
Chambersburg PA
CBHW032303210326
41520CB00047B/903